TEXTUAL AND LITERARY CRITICISM

THE SANDARS LECTURES IN
BIBLIOGRAPHY
1957–58

TEXTUAL & LITERARY CRITICISM

BY

FREDSON BOWERS

Professor of English in the University of Virginia

CAMBRIDGE
AT THE UNIVERSITY PRESS
1966

PUBLISHED BY
THE SYNDICS OF THE CAMBRIDGE UNIVERSITY PRESS

Bentley House, 200 Euston Road, London, N.W.1
American Branch: 32 East 57th Street, New York, N.Y. 10022
West African Office: P.M.B. 5181, Ibadan, Nigeria

First printed   1959
Reprinted   1966
First paperback edition 1966

First printed in Great Britain at the University Press, Cambridge
(Brooke Crutchley, University Printer)
Reprinted by photolithography in the Republic of Ireland
by Browne and Nolan Limited, Dublin

CONTENTS

CONTENTS

PREFACE

THE first three of these lectures on 'Textual and Literary Criticism' were delivered on 20–2 January 1958 in my capacity as Sandars Reader in Bibliography for 1957–8 at Cambridge University. The fourth was given on 23 January 1958 in London before the Bibliographical Society. Since this latter was written very shortly after the completion of the initial series when my mind was much occupied with the general matter, its subject developed naturally from the Sandars lectures and is perhaps best considered in relation to them. I am indebted, therefore, to the Council of the Bibliographical Society for permission to print this fourth paper here rather than separately in the Society's Transactions.

A few excisions made in deference to the patience of my hearers have been restored for the more leisurely reader, and the opportunity has been taken to add some discursive notes to the basic text. Various informalities and acerbities more suitable for speech than for print have been altered; otherwise, the lectures are offered here as in their occasional oral form without other special preparation.

Although the specific subjects of the four discourses present something of a mixed bag, an underlying rationale is intended to be present. Literary criticism is viewed as directly dependent upon expert textual criticism, and some horrid examples are cited to illustrate what can happen when it chooses to operate independently. The expertise of the textual critic is taken as applying to four basic situations: (1) the analysis of the characteristics of an extant manuscript;

(2) the recovery of the characteristics of the lost manuscript that served as copy for a printed text; (3) the study of the transmission of a printed text; and (4) the presentation of the established and edited text to the public.

The first lecture attempts to survey the initial three with illustrations drawn chiefly from post-Renaissance literary works to the present day, both English and American.

The second lecture concerns itself in detail with the first category, using as a case-history a recently investigated group of holograph manuscripts by the American poet Walt Whitman. The unusually full information of particular concern to a literary critic that 'bibliographical' analysis of these manuscripts has yielded, led me to venture a discourse that in its principles was pertinent to the series, though dealing with an author not native to my audience. However, the knowledge that early in his career Whitman was welcomed more boldly in England than in his homeland gave me some cause to hope that he would be an agreeable fellow-countryman to bring across the Atlantic with me.

In the third lecture, devoted exclusively to Shakespeare, some account is given of the most recent textual investigations bearing on the second and third categories, that is, the earnest attempt that is now being made on a new and more scientific basis to recover the essential facts about the copy behind all substantive Shakespeare printed texts, whether single (and thus concerning the identification of manuscript characteristics in the print) or multiple (and thus concerning a scrupulous examination of the circumstances of transmission). Since nothing dates faster these days than Shakespearean textual criticism, the illustrations I have chosen may become obsolete in some respects before this

Preface

book is published; but I hope that the principles enunciated may stand longer than the examples.

The results of textual criticism reach their fruition in an established edited text; and therefore my fourth lecture completes the series by an analysis of the rationale of the modern critical old-spelling edition intended to recover an author's words in their contemporary forms more fully and accurately than can be found in modernised or in facsimile texts, or in any of the original documents.

As they progress, the lectures grow increasingly technical, and emphasis on the factual bases of textual criticism replaces the attention given at the beginning to the factual or rather textual bases of literary criticism. This is a fault for which it is proper to apologise, pleading only the learned auspices of these lectures, the pull of my own special interests, and the particular demands of the subject.

F.B.

CHARLOTTESVILLE, VIRGINIA
20 February 1958

I

TEXTUAL CRITICISM AND
THE LITERARY CRITIC

THE relation of bibliographical and textual investigation to literary criticism is a thorny subject, not from the point of view of bibliography but from the point of view of literary criticism. In contrast to the general uniformity among textual critics about ends and means, literary critics—as we might expect—hold diverse opinions about the operation of their discipline. At one extreme are those higher critics whose chief concern is for the 'total' or 'essential' values of literature, and whose contemplation of an author's work is correspondingly lofty. At the other extreme are critics whose analysis of a work is so detailed that scarcely a word of the text, no matter how ordinary, can escape a searching interpretive inquiry.

In so far as the application of large philosophical and aesthetic concepts to broad problems may dull a critic's awareness of the significance of small details, it is easy for a bibliographer to understand that not all critics may be expected to share his concern for the exactness of representation given to the physical form of the work to be handled. On the other hand, what sometimes seems to be a critic's almost perverse disregard for specific accuracy may offer the bibliographer a nasty shock. Several years ago, in a paper before the English Institute held annually at the invitation of Columbia University, I hoped to stir up some questions and discussion by remarking *inter alia* that I felt

I could prove on physical evidence not subject to opinion that in *Hamlet* Shakespeare wrote 'sallied flesh', and not 'solid flesh'.[1] I confess I was taken aback when the first commentator rose to give it as his opinion that really there ought to be some law to keep bibliographers—who otherwise seemed normal intelligent persons capable of better things—from wasting their lives poking around in such minutiae. Whether Shakespeare wrote 'sallied' (that is, 'sullied') flesh, or 'solid' flesh, was of no importance at all. He personally had read 'solid' all his life, found it quite satisfactory, and saw no reason for changing. Whether it was technically right or wrong did not affect the argument that the Folio phrase had got itself generally accepted. People were used to it. Moreover, the 'essential values' of *Hamlet* the play were not at all affected by retaining the conventional reading here.

Whether this is quite that passion for truth one looks for in a professing critic, I leave aside. I am not really concerned to satirise the 'total values' school and its frequent insensitivity to the actual values of the material on which it chooses to operate; or to invoke laughter at the inadvertencies of the anti-historical 'new critics'. As always, when one is working with a difference in degree, not in kind, the point at which one feels a need to defend the bridge is shifting and uncertain. How many conventional readings in the text of *Hamlet*—one, two, five, ten, twenty, fifty, a hundred, two hundred?—must be proved unsound before the 'total values' of the play *are* affected and the literary critic should begin to grow uneasy about the evidence on which he is formulating his hypothesis for the whole? Because the traditional Old Cambridge text of Shakespeare's

Richard III was based on the bad first quarto instead of the revised good Folio print, current editions can advertise that they contain more than a thousand variants from the conventional text. How many values are affected here?

However, the real danger comes when such a critic—who seems to believe that texts are discovered under cabbage plants (or in bulrushes)—when such a critic tackles a subject in which some knowledge of textual processes is required. For example, in what I understand is—in my country at least—an admired essay on *Lycidas*, John Crowe Ransom argued that Milton, for artistic purposes, deliberately roughed up an originally smooth version of the poem. Characteristically, Ransom made no attempt to examine the transmission of the text from manuscript to print in order to see if there were any physical evidence for his theory. If he had, not only would he have found no support, of course, but evidence to the contrary.[1] How far can we trust the ideas and methods of critics who think so little of analysing the nature of the texts with which they work?

Even scholarly investigators on a less rarefied plane encounter trouble when they ignore textual facts. The identification of Shakespeare's symbolic imagery in play after play has become a popular indoor sport at learned meetings; the study was largely begun by Caroline Spurgeon though she may not be held accountable for the excesses of her imitators. Does it make any difference that some of the images she uses as evidence for her thesis are editorial emendations and not necessarily Shakespeare's words—and that she did not attempt to assess the purity of the evidence she was collecting by using an edition that would show her what was editorial and what not?[2] Does it make any difference

I-2

that the linguist Kökeritz has sometimes used derived instead of primary texts and thus muddied the waters of his evidence;[1] or that when he utilised primary texts for an analysis of Shakespeare's linguistic forms he totally ignored the whole body of bibliographical evidence dealing with facts about variance in different compositors' spelling habits, and, in spite of marked differences in date of printing and in printing-houses, persisted in treating each print of a play, ignoring its origin, as if it were a literally exact transcript of a Shakespearean autograph?[2] Yet this false line of reasoning is basic to his arguments from statistical evidence that such and such forms are Shakespearean spellings. Does it make any difference that even the great *Oxford English Dictionary* has occasionally failed to reproduce an Elizabethan form of a word when it has been ironed out by emendation or modernisation?[3]

We should be seriously disturbed by the lack of contact between literary critics and textual critics. Every practising critic, for the humility of his soul, ought to study the transmission of some appropriate text. If he did, he would raise such an outcry that we should no longer be reading most of the great English and American classics in texts that are inexcusably corrupt. We should no longer complacently accept the sleazy editing that even today too often marks the presentation of works of literature to the student and to the general public.[4]

There is every reason to deplore the common ignorance of textual conditions and of editing standards that puts the critic quite at the mercy of the editor. For example, in 1901 A. H. Thorndike thought that a splendid formula to distinguish the collaborated work of Fletcher from that of

Massinger was the frequent use of the contraction *'em* in Fletcher as against the invariable use of the full form *them* in Massinger.[1] The only trouble was, as he discovered too late, that he had used Gifford's edition of Massinger from which to quarry his evidence; and in this edition Gifford had silently expanded Massinger's *'em* forms to *them*. His edition was untrustworthy, and a man who was at the time an inexperienced scholar—though later a great one—suffered from his misplaced confidence in an improperly edited text.

Fifty years later it is still a current oddity that many a literary critic has investigated the past ownership and mechanical condition of his second-hand automobile, or the pedigree and training of his dog, more thoroughly than he has looked into the qualifications of the text on which his critical theories rest. One may search the history of scholarship in vain to find parallel examples—in relation to the *zeitgeist*—of cultural *naïveté* and professional negligence. Moreover, the danger is not confined to early texts. A critic of *Richard III*, say, who reaches up to his bookshelf and does not care whether he pulls down the Old Cambridge or the New Cambridge volume is no more simple-minded than one who reads Melville or Whitman in texts altered for an English audience, or who—in America—reads most of the Victorians in nineteenth-century American editions,[2] or even T. S. Eliot or Yeats in corrupt American editions instead of the more authentic and often the revised English texts.

Professor R. C. Bald has remarked on the curious fact that as late as 1948 and 1949 respectively, G. B. Harrison and O. J. Campbell, two active and distinguished Shakespearean scholars, put out editions of Shakespeare that were close reproductions of the Old Cambridge, or Globe, text of almost a hundred years before. He adds, 'It is not as if there had been no advances in textual study of Shakespeare during the present century, nor are these two editors ignorant of the work of Pollard, McKerrow, Greg, and Dover Wilson; but is there any other branch of study in which a teacher would be satisfied to present students, as these books do, with the results achieved by scholarship up to, but not beyond, the year 1864?'[1]

If the public, or students and their professors, will not demand good texts, publishers will not offer the means for textual scholars to provide them. Indeed, I have heard it said that Harrison chose to use the Globe text only after his publisher had polled a number of teachers and found the familiar Globe was their preference. I am far from asserting that there is a vast backlog of excellent editions of texts waiting to find a publisher. I am aware that editions of early literature are not considered to be best sellers; and especially if they are in old spelling they may find some serious difficulty in getting into print. I am aware that for too long editing has been esteemed the proper province for the amateur, the pedant, or the dullard who could not even write a biography; and that for too long editing has often deserved its lowly reputation. Moreover, I am conscious that even today the newer editorial methods are only dimly understood by various would-be practitioners. At least, the manuscripts that publishers occasionally send me for an opinion indicate a troubled awareness of the word 'bibliography' though little understanding of its method.

Yet even if we could posit for the future none but ideal

6

editions, I expect there would still remain a considerable isolation of textual bibliographers from their ultimate consumers, the literary critics. This is a pity. I waste no tears on the wounded egos of the bibliographers; the damage is on the other side. I could wish that general critics knew more, and knowing more would care more, about the purity of the texts they use.

In some small part present-day editorial concern with what seem to be relatively minor matters of accurate decision may alienate the critic, such as the one who became impatient at anybody wasting very much time finding out whether Shakespeare wrote *sallied* or *solid*. In this particular case I fancy the choice is important on grounds of meaning, for the word *sullied* supports my contention that Hamlet feels his natural, or inherited, honour has been soiled by the taint of his mother's dishonourable blood. But the weight that may be put on this word is perhaps unusual. For instance, not much is changed whether Hamlet's father's bones were *interred* as in Q2, or *inurned* as in the Folio. Yet I hold it to be an occupation eminently worth while, warranting any number of hours, to determine whether Shakespeare wrote one, or the other, or both. The decision, if clear-cut, might be crucial in the accumulation of evidence whether on the whole the Folio variants from the quarto *Hamlet* are corruptions, corrections, or revisions. If this is a problem no editor has fairly faced, neither should a literary critic be indifferent to the question. Depending upon what can be proved, some hundreds of readings will be affected if an editor decides that Shakespeare revised the text after its second quarto form; for in that case the Folio variants should be chosen in all but the most obvious cases of sophistication. Or he might decide that in only a few cases, where the second quarto compositors have corrupted the text, should the Folio readings take precedence over the generally authoritative second quarto.

True, certain 'values' will not be materially affected one way or the other. Hamlet will not be revealed as a woman, or as the villain; he will still be melancholy and at odds with the life about him. Denmark will still be a prison. Yet what modern author would view with equanimity an edition of one of his plays that substituted several hundred words scattered here and there from the corruptions of typists, compositors, and proof-readers? Not to mention editors. The critic who is so airy about the relation of textual accuracy to 'essential values' would be more touched if an essay of his own were involved in the general corruption.

Nevertheless, I should not wish to rest the case on such a special problem as *Hamlet*. I do not myself think it pedantry to make a fetish of accuracy in scholarship, or in criticism. Only a practising textual critic and bibliographer knows the remorseless corrupting influence that eats away at a text during the course of its transmission. The most important concern of the textual bibliographer is to guard the purity of the important basic documents of our literature and culture. This is a matter of principle on which there can be no compromise. One can no more permit 'just a little corruption' to pass unheeded in the transmission of our literary heritage than 'just a little sin' was possible in Eden.

As a principle, if we respect our authors we should have a passionate concern to see that their words are recovered and currently transmitted in as close a form to their intentions as we can contrive. It should matter to us, as it should matter to all critics, that if one wants to read F. Scott Fitzgerald's *This Side of Paradise* with several of the author's final revisions, one must go to the fourth or later impressions made from plates altered on his instructions, though one must then guard against a proof-reader's error inserted when the plates were unauthoritatively further corrected for the seventh impression.[1]

It should matter to us that in modern reprints of *Tristram Shandy*, to quote an investigator: 'Errors in punctuation amount on many pages to 15 to 20 to the page.... Modern reprints have frequently set in lower case words which Sterne required to be set in small capitals. Alterations in spelling have not been confined to modernizations;... errors destroying Sterne's sense and meaning have been perpetuated, like *area* for *aera*, *clause* for *cause*, *port* for *post*, *timber* for *tinder*, *catching* for *catechising*, and *caravans* for *caverns*.' Many of these errors apparently originated in some popular nineteenth-century reprint, and have been repeated ever since.[2]

I agree with Professor Bald that just critical appraisal is not possible until a text has been established. It should matter to us whether the thirteenth of John Donne's *Holy Sonnets* ends triumphantly, so I say to thee,

> To wicked spirits are horrid shapes assign'd,
> This beauteous forme *assures* a pitious minde

as in Grierson's alteration on manuscript authority, or flatly, as in the printed texts,

> This beauteous forme *assumes* a pitious minde.

It should matter to us that the very bases for establishing the texts of such important Shakespeare plays as

2 *Henry IV*, and *Hamlet*, are still undecided.[1] Until we have the physical facts upon which the establishment of these texts may proceed, no one can quote from such plays with any assurance that he is repeating what Shakespeare intended to write. In the present day it may surprise the complacent to learn that the text of Mr T. S. Eliot's *Murder in the Cathedral*, in respect to his final intentions, is very much in doubt.

I do not say with the classical scholar John Burnet, 'By common consent the constitution of an author's text is the highest aim that a scholar can set before himself'. But I do assert that the establishing of the texts of our literary and historical monuments, and the preservation of their purity through successive processes of transmission, is a task for a scholar of depth, not an employment for the spare hours of a dilettante or the drudgery of a pedant. On the one hand, some textual investigation and recovery calls for creative and imaginative efforts within the discipline of hard fact that compare very favourably indeed, in my opinion, with the broad intellectual powers that often characterised the nineteenth-century literary critic in England, powers that one would like to see still displayed today, on both sides of the Atlantic. On the other hand, bibliography is the only sure foundation on which to rear the necessary wide acquaintance with the whole complex of the past, the intimate knowledge of its thought, the feeling for its idiom, and above all the knowledge of its language for which no amount of enthusiastic dilettante sensibility can adequately compensate, despite the invaluable aid of the *Oxford English Dictionary*.

If we may concede that even the most widely ranging criticism must occasionally descend to exact readings and their interpretation, we must then agree that the critic whose general ideas are in any way related to specific evidence—that is, to the precise details of an author's text—should be most sensitive to the accuracy of that which generates his critical theories.

It is bad enough to have critics disagreeing about whether a great poet's revisions are successful, as—for example—about the altered final lines of Yeats's 'Cuchulain's Fight with the Sea'.[1] One critic maintains that 'The second [ending] is fine too, but has not the same sense of water flowing on and on that is heard in the [first]'. But another writes the exact contrary; for him, the new ending 'transformed a mediocre poem into a work of quite extraordinary power'. Point blank oppositions like these are deplorable, of course. It is worse, however, when a critic is apparently not even conscious that changes of import have taken place. For if we attempt to resolve the above impasse by reference to a third opinion, this one remarks quite blandly, 'The changes do not concern the contents—apart from one small detail: the name Finmole has disappeared'. Obviously we have here a member of the 'total values' school of night, for the revision deleted seven lines and re-did forty-two of the remaining eighty-six, in the process changing the original ending,

> In three days' time, Cuchulain with a moan
> Stood up, and came to the long sands alone:
> For four days warred he with the bitter tide;
> And the waves flowed above him, and he died.

to

>   Cuchulain stirred,
> Stared on the horses of the sea, and heard
> The cars of battle and his own name cried;
> And fought with the invulnerable tide.

We may pass from this example of other-worldliness to the point of real importance: what a literary critic should know about the causes for unsatisfactory or corrupt texts and the processes by which textual critics recover and guard the purity of an author's words. The biblio-textual critic finds that his problems are likely to sort themselves into three major, though not mutually exclusive, categories.

First, when an author's manuscript is preserved, close analysis of the physical characteristics of this manuscript as they bear on the process of composition may yield information of real critical value. Moreover, the preservation of an author's manuscript by no means sets up such an absolute authority as to obviate editorial investigation. If the manuscript is not the exact one used by the printer, a problem in transmission may develop; for revision, or corruption, can enter in the transcripts represented by a secondary manuscript sent to the printer and in the printer's typesetting and proof-reading, with authorial revision always a possibility in the proofs. When, years after publication, we are now able to study the proof sheets of William Faulkner's *Sanctuary* and to learn how a comparatively weak novel was turned into a strong and exciting one by extraordinary revision in proof,[1] we gain a fuller understanding of the structural grasp of a notable artist; and this vital information is secured by observing the pre-publication history of the text between its original and final proof sheets. Yet even if we determine that the translation of author's manuscript into print was normally accomplished, the textual critic cannot be indifferent to the subsequent transmission of the text through various printings and editions.

Secondly, when an author's manuscript has not been

preserved, as is the general rule in literature of the past, an attempt must be made to discover as many as possible of its characteristics in order to estimate the relation of the hypo- thetically reconstructed manuscript to the earliest preserved printed example.

Thirdly, the transmission of a text must be followed with particular scrupulousness in order to sift its variants and assign them to unauthorised changes resulting from the printing process, or to true authorial revisions. This trans- mission may be separated into two parts: first, the stages from manuscript, through various proofs and trials, to actual publication of the first edition in an approved form; and, second, the transmission of the text through various impressions, or printings, as well as through various type- settings, or editions, from the first edition to the present.

In our first category, of manuscripts, I should emphasise that—no matter what the layman may think—an author's manuscript is not always self-sufficient or self-explicatory. For example, the earliest preserved autograph manuscript of Walt Whitman's 'Passage to India', at the New York Public Library, yields some very interesting results to pure bibliographical treatment of it just as a material object.[1] Several early leaves are composed of strips of paper pasted together. By observing the contours of the edges, where they were cut apart, one may reconstruct large portions of the original leaves and thus show what is rearrangement of the earliest level of inscription and what is revision and amplification. Later on, a complete change of paper accom- panies the insertion of an extensive independent poem, 'Oh Soul Thou Pleasest Me'. Then, when 'Passage to

India' continues, the use of substantially the same paper as in the inserted poem instead of the original paper of the earlier part demonstrates that the whole original conclusion (whatever it was) has been revised and copied out fair to take account of the new material that had not at first been contemplated. Earlier, a slight variance in the original paper had accompanied the use of slips of pasted-on proof sheets interspersed with autograph lines. By a somewhat complicated line of reasoning it is possible to show that these proof insertions from two other independent poems were made after the original inscription of the first form of the whole manuscript, but that the addition of the complete poem 'Oh Soul Thou Pleasest Me' was a later operation still, with the consequential revision of the ending, and that this last addition came close to the final stages of the working-over that Whitman gave to the completed manuscript. In some lines one may even distinguish precisely which textual revisions in the added poem were made before the insertion, and which afterwards.

Armed with this information, all of it secured from physical evidence alone, a critic can apply the results to a new understanding of the nature of the poem by his ability to trace the stages of its growth. And in my opinion the critic who neglected this first avenue of approach to understanding would be very foolish indeed. For instance, it is more than a side-issue, in my opinion, that most of the transcendental lines in the poem appear in the late-added 'Oh Soul Thou Pleasest Me'. Any possible imbalance between this section and the earlier original material can thus be accounted for not as a failure in Whitman's compositional inspiration and architectonic vision but as a recasting of preceding lines not perfect enough to lead adequately to the concentration of idea in the insertion.

This is an author's holograph manuscript; yet without what may be called bibliographical analysis most of these facts would not be uncovered or their significance put together into the correct interlocking sequence of reconstruction. If a critic studied this manuscript from photostats, for instance, he would be quite unconscious of most of what I have been elaborating. Author's manuscripts, therefore, are not always the final word unless one can call the author up from the grave to testify about the significance of the physical features. Bibliographers, or their equivalent, are still on occasion needed to make a factual examination and to draw the necessary conclusions before the literary critic can step in.

A critic who becomes impatient at the bibliographer's concern to establish the exact form of a text in all its possible pre-publication states of variance is throwing away, almost wilfully, one of the best possible ways of understanding an author by following him step by step at work. For example, suppose we took the easy attitude—very well, we have the author's earliest manuscript and the first printed edition that presumably contains all the revisions he made. What more do we want? I should say that we lose the opportunity to study the shaping development of idea as represented by stylistic and substantive revision, the manner in which one revision may have given rise to another or to a modification of the initial concept. As in Whitman's 'Passage to India', when one analyses very closely the numerous revisions in the New York Public Library manuscript, especially in their relation to the successive stages of growth in the poem marked by the addition of initially independent material, one learns a great deal about the way Whitman's artistic mind worked. Then if we continue the process, as we should, we may compare the changes made between the final form of the New York Public Library manuscript and the fair copy of it represented by the Harvard manuscript, which was the last holograph before print. But before it was put into type this Harvard manuscript was very considerably revised at different times, in its turn, and a lost early stage of proof—in which a number of changes were made—intervenes between the preserved proof sheets and the final form of the manuscript. Then between this known proof and the printed edition a further twenty-seven alterations appear, including the omission of two whole lines. By a close study of this development of the text up to its first publication we cannot fail to gain an insight into just what Whitman was striving for in the relation of idea to its expression.[1] Most of this evidence would be lost if no more than a simple collation were made of the variants between the earliest or latest form of the New York Public Library manuscript and the printed edition of 1870-1.

Robert Beare, who has made a trial study of the text of T. S. Eliot, came to some interesting conclusions in this matter.[2] After surveying the elimination of punctuation and the deletion of words and phrases to achieve concentration between the pencil holograph and two separate typescripts of 'Marina', preserved in the Bodleian Library, and noting that as late as the very proof copies circulated in advance to reviewers there appeared a line that was deleted only in the actual published state, he concludes, 'The study of the stages of a poem or play which precede publication are of interest and significance for the genesis of the poem rather than as a check of its final published form'. In other words, so many changes can take place between holograph manuscript and first edition that we should study these changes through various transcripts and proofs not for the simple mechanical purpose of checking the accuracy of the printed text (for which the manuscript may or may not be trustworthy in all respects) but instead as an independent act of critical inquiry into the author's mind and art.

And a little later, after a survey of the variants in 'The Waste Land', Beare writes:

There are many incidental gains through approaching an author's work by studying the development of texts of his work. There is the added insight into recurrent phrasing and themes in the poems and plays, and a stricter sense of their chronology and possible relationships. In Eliot's poetry there is also room to discuss under variants the alterations in phrasing which borrowings from other authors have undergone. Again, unless we have the sense of the actual chronology of the works, we cannot discuss influences in their proper perspectives, such as the possible influence of Joyce on 'The Waste Land' through the serialization of *Ulysses*.

If anyone inquires what all this has to do with the independent life of the poem as we have it in the form that the author wanted to present to the world, I think we can answer that we are likely to know an adult better if we have followed him through all the stages of his childhood. Though a poem, like a man, may stand rejoicing in finished maturity, we must surely understand it with superior intimacy if we have watched its growth and seen its perfection in the very act of shaping. There is such a thing as love, I should urge, in our response to a perfect poem. The current games of intellectual chess, of subjectively drawn tensions, ambiguities, and *discordia concors*, too often overlook or overlay that simple act of love, which the textual critic may help us toward in his concern for the childhood and adolescence, awkward or charming, of the living seed of a writer.

We may turn to the second category in which bibliotextual problems cluster: the attempt to recover as many as possible of the characteristics of an author's lost manuscript from the evidence of the earliest printed edition related to the manuscript. Here we come to a very broad area of textual bibliography which is devoted, often in a highly technical manner, to estimating the effect of scribal transcript or of compositorial typesetting on the author's lost original. Textual critics of biblical, classical, and medieval manuscripts have developed to a relatively high point the art of recovering details of the lost original and of reconstructing a synthetic text that is superior to any single preserved form. In later periods, the more strictly bibliographical investigation of the effect of the printing process on an author's text is in its early stages, and its results are at present only provisional. I shall have something to say on this point when in my third chapter I come to textual studies of Shakespeare; my remarks now must be taken as being in their turn quite provisional.

Ordinarily it is true that the nearer one comes to modern times, the more difficulty one has in penetrating the veil of print and recovering the characteristics of the lost manuscript. The uniformity of compositorial usage, added to the strong-minded styling given a typescript by the publisher's reader before setting, at the present day has a marked tendency to impose standard characteristics of syntax, punctuation, spelling, and sometimes of phrasing, on an author's individuality of expression. Yet we must not over-estimate these forces, powerful as they are in smoothing out individualities found in an author's manuscript. Louis N. Feipel, whose hobby was proof-reading printed books, supplied Harcourt, Brace with a list of about a hundred inconsistencies and errors in the first printing of Sinclair Lewis's novel *Babbitt.* To which Lewis commented in awe, 'This man Feipel is a wonder—to catch all these after rather unusually careful proofreading not only by myself and my wife but also by two or three professionals'. Even so, Lewis showed himself uncertain of the meaning of *B* in *B.P.O.E.* since he twice gave it in error as *Brotherly* and only once correctly as *Benevolent* (*B.P.O.E.* is the abbreviation for an American fraternal society, The Benevolent and Protec-tive Order of Elks). And Lewis's spelling of *Oddfellows* and *Redmen* (two similar orders) as one word instead of two is not quite the way in which these organisations choose to denominate themselves. The mordant satirist of American 'joiners' and their groups did not, on the evidence, always have a keen eye for such details in the objects of his laughter.[1]

The various misspellings and inaccuracies that crept into the references to proper names in Fitzgerald's *This Side of Paradise*, and were only partly rooted out by successive alterations of the plates, provide some evidence of his care-lessness, vagueness, and even ignorance. Indeed, it is clear that when one collates the text of successive impressions of modern books, the various alterations that may be detected in the plates are often indications of original aberrancies repeated direct from the authors' manuscripts. It is amusing at the very least to know that despite his considerable display of erudition, James Branch Cabell—another American novelist—had frequently to correct his Latin in second impressions, and sometimes his French. Cabell, like Fitzgerald and Lewis, also took such occasions to make textual revisions in the plates, as well as corrections.[1]

I am sorry that my best modern illustration of the application of bibliography to recover the features of a manuscript appears to be hypothetical. At least, no one else present on the occasion agrees with my memory that I was shown a second edition of a modern English poet. In this second edition were four to six lines in an altered version that seemed patently inferior to the version in the first edition. The problem was—did this author revise for the worse, or could a bibliographical explanation be evolved? I suggested that an explanation was indeed possible. The book had been printed in England and therefore almost certainly had been set in Monotype. Monotype is set by punching a paper-tape roll that is subsequently run through a caster that automatically sets the type. If a second impression is much delayed, and the book has not been plated, the type can be distributed in the interval, since for a second printing all one need do is run the tape through the caster again to secure an exact duplicate of the first-impression typesetting. Of course, the publisher must carefully repeat all the stages of corrected proofs, or conflate them into one; for *all* proof changes made in the first typesetting must be repeated by hand in the second. If, as was possible, the revision of the lines in question had been made at a late stage and there had been a slip-up in preserving or conflating these proofs, the situation would be brought about that the first printing had given us the revised lines but the second printing the original lines before revision. The last would have been first here with a vengeance. The illustration is so neat that it is a pity it is very likely not true. Observe, of course, that the explanation would not fit if the book had been printed in America where Linotype is ordinarily used for commercial printing: under these conditions a second printing could be made only from standing type or from plates; and there would be no possible way in which the types of the original reading could reappear, as in Monotype.

As a sidenote on the importance of knowing the process of printing, and its effect on the transmission of texts, we may observe that the excision of a line from Eliot's *The Rock* in the Harcourt, Brace printing is not an instance of authorial initiative but instead the result of a bad splice made in the negative for the American photo-offset edition.

Sometimes quite mechanical evidence can be brilliantly used to recover facts about a lost manuscript. Professor Donald Bond observed that the folio first-edition issues of the *Spectator* papers kept headlines, rules, and advertisements in standing type, but that a curious alternation existed between the complete sets of such standing material. When he further associated each set of standing types with certain spelling peculiarities, he was able to demonstrate that two printers, Buckley and Tonson, alternated in producing the *Spectator* papers in order to allow enough time for sufficient quantities to be printed without duplicate composition. He thereupon observed that of the papers readily attributable to Addison the vast majority were printed by Tonson; and of the papers attributable to Steele the vast majority were printed by Buckley; and he further observed that this assignment was invariable after a certain point. Not only could unidentified work of these two men be assigned to the correct authorship on this evidence; but the work of contributors who were closely associated either with Addison or with Steele could also be allocated to Tonson or to Buckley on the same basis. Hence ranges of lost manuscript could be identified on merely mechanical printing evidence.[1]

In an earlier period Dr Cyrus Hoy observed that compositors were generally faithful enough to small details of contractions, so the collaborated work of Beaumont, Fletcher, Massinger, Shirley, Rowley, and Field can be identified by small linguistic patterns peculiar to each author, like the use of *'em* for *them*, of *i'th* for *in the*, or of *o'th* for *of the*, and so on. This identification, moreover, could sometimes be carried to such a state of refinement that Dr Hoy could offer evidence as to the exact status of the manuscript for some plays, whether the holograph of different authors, or a fair copy by one author of his own and his collaborator's scenes, or a scribal transcript of both.[2] In a recent article another scholar, Dr Frederick Waller, has shown from physical evidence the strong possibility that Fletcher touched up in various specific places several of the scenes customarily assigned to Shakespeare in *The Two Noble Kinsmen*.[3]

Characteristics of the printed texts have for some time revealed excellent reason for assigning the manuscripts of some Elizabethan plays to the scribe Ralph Crane; whereas other evidence relating to the punctuation of stage-directions in some plays has suggested that the printer's manuscript was a transcript by Edward Knight, book-keeper for the King's Men.

Indeed, my own experience with *The Virgin Martyr*, a play printed in 1622, indicates that despite some difficulties the manuscript behind the first edition was very likely not a scribal copy but instead the assembled autograph papers of the two authors, Massinger and Dekker. For this play the separate spelling habits of the two authors come through the typesetting by a single compositor with sufficient clarity to make this hypothesis plausible, and join with certain linguistic traits to settle the authorship of the scenes in this collaboration on better evidence than stylistic impressions. In fact, the evidence is such that it is possible to conjecture that in at least one scene, and perhaps two, of the fourth act, Dekker copied over original Massinger composition in the course of amplifying and revising the scene.[1]

The significance of such studies as I have mentioned, and the means by which the evidence is brought together and analysed, I propose to discuss more fully in the third lecture on Shakespearean textual criticism.

In the third category, the transmission of a text may pose serious problems for a literary critic, all the more serious in that he is ordinarily quite unaware that such problems exist. In more spacious days it was customary for dilettante editors, unacquainted with the rigours of textual criticism, to reprint the last edition of a text issued in the author's lifetime. The reason alleged was that this edition—in ordinary circumstances—would be the last that an author might have revised. It rarely occurred to such editors that they were under an obligation to show whether or not the author had in truth revised the edition chosen. The possibility was taken as sufficient warrant. As a result, without any determination of authority, all the accumulated corruptions from successive reprintings were carefully reproduced by editors as if, tacitly, they were authorial variants—no attempt being made to sort out and to analyse the relation of the different editions to each other and, on the evidence, to determine whether at any point fresh authority had intervened. For example, when in 1868 Henry Morley came to re-edit the *Spectator* papers, he estimated that some three thousand textual corruptions had accumulated in the last standard edition.⟩

The transmission of texts, and what happens in this transmission, is a subject of particular fascination, worth a discourse in itself instead of the very few examples I can devote to it. Although the last-edition-in-the-author's-lifetime formula no longer holds the estimation formerly accorded it, a reaction that exalts the first edition at the expense of all others can be dangerous too. Only when the transmission of a text has been carefully studied, and each edition after the first established firmly as a mere reprint without authority, can an editor rely wholly on the first edition, after due regard for its misprints. Otherwise, whenever revision is established in any later edition, editorial procedures of some delicacy may be involved, and the bibliographical facts become paramount as the basis for general as well as specific decision.

The new edition of Goldsmith by Professor Friedman, and the new edition of the *Spectator* papers by Professor Bond, both now in their final stages of preparation, should provide badly needed models for the editing of eighteenth-century texts, a field that has usually been one of the disgraces of scholarship.

Shortly after the *Spectator* first-edition folio had been

completed, an edition in octavo was announced, and a cheaper edition in duodecimo was printed, in great part simultaneously with the octavo. Collation establishes just about every possible form of revision and transmission. In some cases (when there was alteration) the folio papers were revised for the octavo, but in others not for the octavo but for the duodecimo. In some cases the duodecimo follows uncorrected folio sheets, in others corrected folio sheets, in some the octavo sheets, in others octavo sheets annotated with revisions. After careful study of the transmission an editor will in each case choose the folio as copy-text, following Greg's classic advice to select as one's basis the printed edition that was set up directly from manuscript; but when variants in readings appear he will choose some from the folio, some from the octavo, and others from the duodecimo, this choice depending not—as customarily—on mere intuition but instead quite rigorously on what the evidence of transmission has shown to be the particular pages of a particular edition set from the most authoritative revised copy.[1]

From the nineteenth century I select as an interesting case the text of Shelley's *Posthumous Poems*. These were first printed in 1824 by Mrs Shelley, who edited them again, revised, in the collection of 1839. Modern editors have contented themselves with reprinting the presumed authoritative text of 1839 without inquiring into the history of its transmission; and in so doing they have perpetuated a number of errors by their negligence. Briefly, the story is this. In copies sold very late in 1824 an important errata leaf containing twenty-four corrections was bound in; but this leaf is so rare as to have escaped general knowledge. The 1824 poems were promptly pirated, and piracies were

made of the piracies, most of which had not used the errata-
leaf corrections. When Mrs Shelley came to re-edit the
poems for the 1839 collection, by bad luck she did not
choose as printer's copy the 1824 edition, but instead took
one of the piracies of a piracy, though—by good fortune
this time—the text (even if sometimes corrupt) had printed
most but not all of the errata-leaf variants. Mrs Shelley,
of course, had quite forgotten about the errata leaf by 1839.
Although she made a fresh comparison of the print with the
manuscripts in her possession, as one would expect she
missed three of the late but important errata-leaf corrections
and allowed various of the piracy's accumulated corruptions
to stand; and these, as a consequence, appeared in her 1839
text, to be copied by all subsequent editors as authoritative
readings. This is true *naïveté*, which a study of the transmission would long since have exposed if any editor had
troubled to make the inquiry, before Dr Charles Taylor's
Yale dissertation worked out the problem.[1]

There should be no complacency about our modern texts.
The plates of a book may be altered without notice in any
impression, yet the latest printing from altered plates is not
necessarily the most correct. For example, Sinclair Lewis's
novel *Babbitt* had two sets of plates made in 1922 from the
original typesetting after proof-correction. The first set of
plates printed the first to the fourth impressions. In the
first impression we have two readings corrected in a rare
example of modern stop-press alteration of plates. Six more
readings were changed in the plates for the second impression,
and thirteen more in the fourth. However, after 1942 all
printings were made from the second set of plates; but
these had not been carefully kept up-to-date with the altera-

tions made in the first plates and hence all printings from 1942 to the present day revert in fourteen out of twenty-one cases to original first-impression errors that had been corrected either in the second or the fourth impressions. A critic who uses any other printing of *Babbitt* than the fourth may quote a passage that in some detail does not correspond to certain of Lewis's revised intentions.[1]

In *Babbitt* the consequences may not be very serious, except in principle. But one never knows when an error in modern texts will rise to plague a critic who is not aware of the transmission of the text he is using. A good example of utter confusion is illustrated by Delmore Schwartz, writing about Yeats's poem 'Among School Children'. Schwartz was aware that the reading 'Soldier Aristotle' was new in the 1933 American edition of the *Collected Poems* instead of the older reading 'Solider Aristotle'; but he felt helpless to determine whether it was or was not a misprint. Hence he circled about the subject gingerly, interpreting the fifth stanza in two ways depending upon whether one reads 'Soldier' or 'Solider' Aristotle. He is not very happy about his results, since 'Soldier' imports the wars of Alexander rather unbecomingly into a poem about school-children, but what else he can do he does not know.

His comments are instructive. 'The whole problem of the meaning or meanings of any poem is raised by this example', he writes, '... but in one form or another much of Yeats's verse raises the same questions for any reader, namely, what are the limits which define legitimate interpretation? Are there any limits?'

The answer he finds puzzling. Quite rightly he rejects the Empsonian attitude that the more simultaneous interpretations one can give to a poem the better. He also rejects, though more reluctantly, the thesis that an interpretation is valid if it is consistent with the whole context of the poem taken as a literal statement. Again, because he cannot reconcile the divergent meanings of 'Soldier Aristotle' and 'Solider Aristotle', he feels this criterion will not operate. Thereupon he gives up the quest, and goes over completely to something like mysticism:

Whatever the answer to the whole problem of interpretation or this particular instance of it may be [he writes], this problem and all the problems...should add up to a definition of ignorance. Yet this defined ignorance assumes, knows, and depends upon an inexhaustible substance like Life itself. Only admiration of this substance could bring one to a concern with its problems and mysteries. It is with this admiration, with a conviction of the greatness of this poetry, that our author will begin and end. All will begin and end with admiration and love of the greatness of this poetry.[1]

I submit that we may feel admiration and love for the greatness of poetry without having a critic ask us to admire and love a misprint that he has failed to recognise as an error. This peroration seems to me to be high-faluting nonsense. Humility before a great work of art is a proper attitude. But to exalt ignorance of the principles of textual criticism into admiration of the protoplasmic mysteries of Life (with a capital L) is more than we should be willing to stomach.

One could carry on indefinitely with such examples. Mr Beare quotes Eliot's lines from *Ash Wednesday*:

> And the light shone in darkness and
> Against the Wor[l]d the unstilled world whirled
> About the centre of the silent Word.

He comments: 'The "1" which found its way into "Word" has persisted through every subsequent printing of the *Collected Poems*, every selection from it, including the new *Selected Poems* of a year or so ago, [it is] in every foreign translation, and I remember seeing these lines used once somewhere as an example of the difficulty of interpreting Eliot's poetry.'

Even when authors cultivate ambiguity of expression, critics should be particularly careful to view the text with some caution before giving the devil more than his due. On page 29 of the first English printing of *The Cocktail Party* occurs a misprint in the earlier copies from the press, though corrected part way through the run. The un-identified guest, in the corrected version, replies to Edward's statement that he wants to see Lavinia again:

> You shall see her again—here.

This is sufficiently portentous, but the earlier printed line reads, in error,

> You shall see here again—here.

We may look forward with apprehension, perhaps, to reading some day a metaphysical discourse on Eliot's view of time and the nature of reality, as expressed in the pregnant line, 'You shall see here again—here'.

Criticism of modern literature as if it were written by seventeenth-century 'metaphysicals' has produced various admirable treatises, but sometimes the approval of *discordia concors* is carried to the lengths of extravagant praise for the *discordia* of a printer's error without the *concors* of the poet's intention. Such an instance is found in F. O. Matthiessen's discussion of a phrase of Herman Melville's in *White-Jacket*. Melville is describing his fall into the sea from the yard-arm

of the U.S. frigate *Neversink*. In the Constable Standard
Edition of Melville's *Works* we read the following description
of his feelings as he floats under water in an almost trance-
like state:

I wondered whether I was yet dead or still dying. But of
a sudden some fashionless form brushed my side—some inert,
soiled fish of the sea; the thrill of being alive again tingled in
my nerves, and the strong shunning of death shocked me through.

Commenting on these lines Matthiessen writes:

But then this second trance is shattered by a twist of imagery
of the sort that was to become peculiarly Melville's. He is
startled back into the sense of being alive by grazing an inert
form; hardly anyone but Melville could have created the shudder
that results from calling this frightening vagueness some 'soiled
fish of the sea.' The *discordia concors*, the unexpected linking of
the medium of cleanliness with filth, could only have sprung
from an imagination that had apprehended the terrors of the
deep, of the immaterial deep as well as the physical.

The only difficulty with this critical *frisson* about Melville's imagination, and undemonstrable generalisations such
as 'nobody but Melville could have created the shudder',
and so on, is the cruel fact that an unimaginative typesetter
inadvertently created it, not Melville; for what Melville

wrote, as is demonstrated in both the English and American
first editions, was *coiled* fish of the sea.[1] It is disheartening
to find the enthusiasm of critics so easily betrayed; just as
it is disheartening to find sensible critics defending with their
heart's blood a Yeats misspelling or misprint in the *disdain-
distain* controversy from 'Byzantium' that enlivened the
pages of *The Times Literary Supplement* in 1950.[2] Although
I deplore the national allusion, I have some sympathy with
the disgust of the correspondent Mr John Christopherson

who midway in the discussion (*T.L.S.* 1950, p. 581) declared roundly that Yeats was a notoriously bad speller, and this was the sole explanation for the error *distain*; and continued, in criticism of earlier letters on the subject, 'Such barren discussion and dissection as is at present being carried on in America and elsewhere is no doubt what Yeats himself had in mind when he spoke of pedants "coughing in ink"'. I do not myself object to word-mongering so violently as Mr Christopherson, nor do I recognise it as so palpably characteristic of my country's critical habits as he chooses to believe; nevertheless, I am sure we should agree that it is indeed somewhat indicative of the over-subtlety of our times, even of our international times, to find the complexities of a misprint so eloquently preferred to the relative simplicity of the author's own phrase.

In the matter of finding preferential literary excellences in misprints Professor Empson is a frequent offender by reason of his careless use of imperfect texts, complicated by a more than ordinary inaccuracy of quotation from these texts. I can only mention in passing his gaffe in *Seven Types of Ambiguity* in which he argues most persuasively for an added eeriness in Eliot's 'Whispers of Immortality' caused by the slight doubt about the syntax in the tenth, eleventh, and twelfth lines (a doubt materially aided by his punctuating of the twelfth line in a way not found in any Eliot text). In fact, on the ambiguity of the syntax he ultimately comes to the position that 'This I take to be the point of the poem, and it is conveyed by the contradictory ways of taking the grammar'.

Well, when a critic arrives at conclusions about the point of a poem that are reached through the interpretation of printer's errors in the text, we may see how readily white may be made black, and black white, and we may be forgiven if we treat his opinions in general with some reserve. The truth is that Empson studied Eliot, and spun his finely drawn theories about Eliot's literary art, not from the relatively pure first or second editions, but from either the third or the fourth edition. By bad luck a printer's common transpositional error in the third edition exchanged the terminal punctuation of lines 10 and 11, making the end of the sentence come at line 10 instead of line 11, and wrongly beginning a new sentence with the final infinitive phrase of the correct old sentence; and the mistake was not caught up until the sixth edition. On the evidence of the periodical text of the poem, followed by its first two book editions, and the correction of the sixth edition, it was the faulty printer—and not the poet—who introduced the syntactical ambiguity that Empson so greatly admired and felt was the point of the whole poem. I should dearly like to know whether Eliot blushed, or laughed, when he read Empson on this poem and its non-existent point.

Nevertheless, this example illustrates a real problem; and Empson might well have felt aggrieved at the original slip on Eliot's part when he passed the punctuation error, for some revisions in this poem indicate that the poet had overlooked these verses when making some changes for the third edition.

I conclude with an anecdote that has its pertinence.

Some years ago a visiting lecturer was to speak on Eliot at the University of Virginia, and for the occasion a little complimentary programme was printed, containing the text of 'Gerontion'. Our then curator of rare books consulted the 1936 Harcourt, Brace *Collected Poems*, which was conveniently at hand, and, being a man of conscience, also looked at a few earlier editions to check the text. When he began turning up variants, he then amused himself by constructing an eclectic text. Subsequently, the late Peters Rushton showed this text to Mr Eliot at a luncheon and pointed out a few of the differences, but unfortunately not all the twenty-one variants that had developed between 1919 and 1936. Eliot checked some in confirmation, and altered two. Presumably he thereupon approved of the text in the form he really wanted it; but if so, he passed over one obvious misprint in the programme lines, and approved a text that in all its details conforms to no printed edition. In a few cases he approved an earlier reading which had been changed in a revised edition; in others, he approved the revision.[1]

The moral as I see it, here and in the Empson case, is this. If a literary critic is going to do much with fine points of text, even though he escape 'barren discussion and dissection', he would be very well advised (lacking a truly scholarly edition of his author) to make some independent investigation into the transmission and what it shows before he bases, in print, an assertion about 'the whole point of a poem' on small matters of ambiguous punctuation, syntax, or even—as with 'Soldier Aristotle' or 'Against this World'—individual words. A revised edition of a modern author (as of an earlier one) is no guarantee that errors in transmission from preceding editions will not be perpetuated in the printer's copy; and the author's approval of the real revisions in an edition cannot be made to cover every exact detail. Revisions will very likely exist side by side with corruptions resulting from the new typesetting or passed on from earlier editions.

The literary critic must become sophisticated, and leave his childish faith in the absoluteness of the printed word. Before he expatiates upon subtle ambiguities and two-way syntax he had better check his facts, that is to say his text. This problem of the text of a modern author is in some respects more acute than with older writers.[1] Problems in transmission are no less prevalent, and revising authors like James,[2] Yeats, and Eliot may baffle the critic about the form of the text to be preferred, as with *Murder in the Cathedral.* The latest author-revised edition of a modern writer is, I should say, often less trustworthy than a scholarly edition of an older author. Paradoxically, a critic quoting from an uncomplicated Shakespearean text is more likely to be closer to his author's full intentions, so far as these can be ascertained, than he is in quoting Yeats—unless he is very careful indeed about his editions.

In the one case, whether he appreciates it or not, he can rely on a certain amount of enlightened textual criticism to have provided him with a trustworthy text. For most modern authors, however, he is—unfortunately—on his own; and the eclipse in which he often wanders may find a suitable commentary in the lines that Empson darkened instead of illuminated by finding eeriness and ambiguity in their syntax:

> Donne, I suppose, was such another
> Who found no substitute for sense
> To seize and clutch and penetrate.

The kind of *sense* that Mr Eliot is imputing here to John Donne differs from the kind I have been advocating in this lecture, however, for I should like to prefix to my kind the simple adjective—*common.*

THE WALT WHITMAN MANUSCRIPTS
OF 'LEAVES OF GRASS' (1860)

ONE of the difficulties facing the serious critic of American literature is the unpredictability of the primary source materials on which textual and literary investigation must depend. These materials, especially the precious manuscripts, are widely scattered and so frequently preserved, uncatalogued and unknown, in the hands of private collectors, that any scholar who needs to follow their traces must keep an active card file of auction records and purchases. Surprises, though not an everyday occurrence, may always be expected.

One afternoon early in the September of 1951, the noted collector of American literature, C. Waller Barrett, spread before my eyes the contents of a thick leather case packed full with autograph manuscripts by Walt Whitman. It seemed incredible that these manuscripts of about eighty poems could have existed so many years after Whitman's death without scholarly notice or curiosity save in one small instance. That they did so, and that these literary riches are now available for critical use in an edition,[1] is the sole excuse for concerning myself here with a subject so far removed from my ordinary experience. It was an honour to have been invited to edit these manuscripts; and despite its inevitable drudgery the experience itself was fascinating. Not only did these papers represent the largest group of Whitman's poetic manuscripts in existence, all but one of them unreproduced, but they offered the opportunity for literary detective work at various levels of criticism that was of the highest interest to attempt.

I shall describe some of this detective work and how it proved possible to draw an astonishing number of conclusions about these manuscripts by inductions based on their physical evidence. But facts are not much use without interpretation; hence I shall remark—however briefly— some of the significance that these manuscripts have for our understanding of Walt Whitman. This significance is two-fold. First, there are some unknown biographical facts contained in the manuscripts and their interpretation— personal as well as literary biography. Second, they show that many current views of Whitman as a literary artist are mistaken.

For the first, whatever the literary historian can discover about Whitman's life during the years 1857–60 is especially valuable, since the poet destroyed most of the personal memoranda that he made in these years. These manuscripts were all written between 1857 and 1860, and since in many respects their first printed form differs from that in the original manuscript version, some few personal facts emerge that would otherwise be lost.

More significant are facts about what we may call Whitman's literary biography. The first edition of *Leaves of Grass* in 1855, with only twelve poems, for all its revolutionary idiom was in many respects a poor thing. And the second edition of 1856, increased to thirty-two poems, was not a great deal better. Suddenly in 1860—in the third edition —we have an outpouring of about a hundred and thirty poems with a maturity and liveness in the writing that had not been matched before and was only to be matched later in a few inspired poems. This third edition, on the word of recent critics, is the most significant of all the *Leaves of Grass*. And these manuscripts show the literary growth of this edition through the three secret years, facts about its growth that are completely concealed in the printed form and were never mentioned by Whitman. Such revelations are important.

Equally important, though perhaps less immediately interesting, is the record these manuscripts contain of the slow, careful initial composition and then the scrupulous revision that Whitman gave his poems. Whitman liked to suggest that his verse flowed from him in a natural outpouring. Some critics have, indeed, been deceived into accepting this picture. For example, in a collection of critical studies published recently, William Carlos Williams writes as follows: 'Whitman didn't have the training to construct his verses after a conscious mold which would have given him power over them to turn them this way, then that, at will. He only knew how to give them birth and to release them to go their own way.'[1]

This romantic concept proves to be quite misleading. The manuscripts show Whitman casting and recasting his lines sometimes six and seven times, trying out words in different combinations in layer after layer of revision. The picture of Whitman as Fancy's child, warbling his native woodnotes wild, is as false as it was for Shakespeare. In their original composition, and then subsequently for almost three years, Whitman worked and re-worked the poems that were to make up the 1860 edition. If one still does not like the result, one can assert—if one chooses—that Whitman is indeed a bad poet if he could do no better after all that effort. But no one can any longer say that Whitman gave these poems birth and then released them to go their own way. He licked them into shape like the legendary mother bear forming her cubs. And in this process, Mr Williams to the contrary, he knew what he was doing and was able to control his results.

Now, for the first time, an interested critic can see Whitman truly in the workshop. In line after line he can analyse the alterations that developed parallelism as a rhetorical device, that constantly sought words of sharper meaning, that wed meaning to cadence in experiments with alliteration, with increased melodiousness and subtly juxtaposed strongly-accented monosyllables with undulating words of greater length and flexibility. Whitman was a conscious literary artist. Poetic composition did not, I think, come very easily to him. His first thoughts are seldom more than crude sketches for the finished edifice, and often they are scarcely recognisable in the final result. These poems were built, for all their air of carefree extemporaneousness. In this, as in so many other of his characteristics, Whitman succeeded in imposing on the world the persona that he wanted to be accepted by posterity as well as by his contemporaries.

So much for the general background of the manuscripts and their significance. Now let us look at the papers themselves and their problems.

When Waller Barrett bought these manuscripts, an oral tradition accompanied them that they had come from the shop of Rome Brothers, a Brooklyn printing firm run by friends of Whitman; and indeed the shop in which, according to report, Whitman had himself set the type for the first edition of *Leaves of Grass* in 1855. This tradition was, at least in part, substantiated by the word of the Whitman scholar, Emory Holloway, who had seen these manuscripts before 1921, when they were in the possession of Patrick Valentine, and had reported finding among them a now lost letter from T. H. Rome to their original purchaser, a book- and autograph-dealer named Benjamin. It was not until 1954, however, that by pure chance I came upon a printed broadside in a Whitman collection recently deposited in the New York Public Library that proved to be the sales list advertising these manuscripts for sale by Rome Brothers. Many of the manuscripts are named by title in this list, and a few are mentioned that are not now contained in the collection. This sales list authenticated the origin of the papers, and established the dating for a few of the manuscripts not now preserved save in the 1860 printed form.

On the other hand, Rome Brothers did not print the third edition, which was manufactured in Boston for the publishers Thayer and Eldridge. How, then, did Rome Brothers come to possess them? Comparison of the text of the manuscripts with the finally printed form of 1860 frequently showed a range of variation too marked and too extensive to be ascribed merely to correction in proof. Fortunately, just about this time, in the Harvard library I came upon a Whitman manuscript for the later 'Passage to India', accompanied by a letter to Rome Brothers from Whitman enclosing ten dollars and asking them to set the poem in type for him and to send him corrected galleys. The galleys were also preserved at Harvard, and from these it was clear that the poem, as eventually printed in the 1871 *Leaves*, was in a quite different typesetting from the galleys. More-over, the manuscript for 'Passage to India', though mostly autograph, had some lines pasted in on printed pieces of paper. One set of these I recognised as printed versions of a few lines from a poem called 'Fables' that was also in the Barrett manuscripts. The pieces of the jigsaw puzzle fitted into place. It was clear that Whitman was accustomed to sending his poems to be set by a printer after they had reached a certain stage of composition, as today a poet might send his handwritten papers to a typist. Just so, Whitman must have sent his third-edition poems to Rome Brothers for typesetting and proofs; and at some subsequent time had used these proofs, heavily revised and rewritten in many cases, and sometimes greatly enlarged by fresh com-position, to send to Boston as printer's copy for his third edition.

The printed slips of paper containing lines from the Rome Brothers' proof of 'Fables' (of later date) in 'Passage to India' was a perfect example of the extreme revision and expansion that a poem might undergo, sometimes even being built up from parts of originally quite independent poems.

The identification of the manuscripts not as the printer's copy for the third edition but instead as the manuscripts behind a lost typesetting that in revised form served as printer's copy had important implications. First, it showed that a further intensive round of revision had intervened between the final form of the manuscripts and the final form of the printer's copy. Moreover, although these worked-over Rome Brothers' proofs that served as printer's copy were lost, all the changes that Whitman made in them could be recovered merely by comparing the final manuscript version of the poems against the printed edition, with allowance for only normal proof-reading. Thus the important last layer of revision could be completely isolated for study, and certain limits could be set to the dating of this important last round of revision and amplification.

Second, these facts would be useful in considering certain poems found only in the 1860 edition. There are twenty-seven of these new poems printed in 1860 but not present either in the Barrett manuscripts or in the Rome Brothers' sales list. It is quite clear, I think, that these twenty-seven represent poems composed between the date when Whitman sent his manuscripts to be set and proofed by Rome Brothers and the date (about 1 March 1860) when he dispatched printer's copy to Boston. Thus the critic has isolated for his inspection the twenty-seven last-composed poems of the 1860 edition. It is of some interest, I suggest, that of these poems six occur in the Enfans d'Adam section, and nine in the Calamus section. Thus over half of these late poems went into two important 1860 sections, what Whitman called 'clusters', the one celebrating heterosexual love and the other what Whitman called 'manly love', or comradeship, a theme that bulks large in the 1860 edition and one that is considerably illuminated by these manuscripts.

At this point of the investigation it was clear that a maximum effort had to be made to date these manuscripts. At the upper end the dates for the 1860 edition were fixed. We have the original letter in the Charles Feinberg collection in which on 10 February 1860 Thayer and Eldridge first offered to print his third edition; and in the same collection is another of 27 February stating that the publishers are prepared to start work at once. Printer's copy was very likely delivered shortly after 1 March, therefore. Whitman went to Boston during the second week of March to start reading proof, and the book was published in late April or early May.

On the other hand, the development of the third edition from its beginnings was by no means so clearly delineated. The second edition of the *Leaves* had been announced in August of 1856 and was issued in September. There is evidence that immediately after—and almost certainly even before—Whitman had begun to plan and indeed to work on a greatly expanded third edition. For example, in Chants Democratic no. 4, a poem known in manuscript under the title 'Feuillage', the version printed in 1860 reads at verse 7, 'The Area the Eighty-third year of These States—the three and a half millions of square miles', etc. This sounds as though the poem were written in 1859; but when we consult the manuscript we read, 'The area the Eightieth year of These States—the three millions of square miles'. The eightieth year of the United States would be 1856; and from this reference it would seem that the poem was at least drafted in that year. Another reference occurs in the 1860 poem entitled 'Proto-Leaf', a poem that later became 'Starting from Paumanok'. In a passage not in the manuscript (and therefore one written in late 1859) the 1860 text reads,

> In the Year 80 of The States,
> My tongue, every atom of my blood, formed from this
>   soil, this air,
> Born here of parents born here,

42

> From parents the same, and their parents' parents
> the same,
> I, now thirty-six years old, in perfect health, begin,
> Hoping to cease not till death.

This is a dedication to his lifework, the construction of a great series of prophetic poems of which the 1855 and 1856 *Leaves of Grass* had been but faint adumbrations. The mention of the eightieth year of the United States establishes the date as 1856; but in 1856 Whitman was aged thirty-six only between 1 January and 30 May. Thus it would seem that when these lines were written in 1859, Whitman was looking back dramatically to the months in 1856 when what must have been an extraordinary vision had come to him, a vision of the book that he was later to call the 'New Bible' for mankind, a book that was to dwarf the feeble beginnings of the 1855 edition, and the second edition, also, that was already at that time in the last stage of preparation.

That this vision in the late winter or early spring of 1856 was shortly implemented is shown by a notebook in the Feinberg collection in which Whitman began to draft the opening lines for the first poem in the new edition, to be called 'Proem'. This notebook is dated October 1856. On one of its pages Whitman writes a note about the poem. 'The Proem must have throughout a strong saturation of America, The West, the Geography, the representative American man.' Its first line was, originally, 'Preface of Endless Announcements', followed by

> Toward the perfect woman of America,
> Toward the perfect man of America,
> Toward the President of These States, and the
> members of the Congress of These States.

Shortly we find the title changed to 'Premonition', and a new opening,

> To you, endless announcements
> Whoever you are, For your sake these.

Then these opening lines are given a note that they should become the last verse of the poem, and a new beginning starts to take shape:

> Free, savage, strong,
> Cheerful, luxuriant, fluent, self-composed, fond of
>   friends, fond of women and children,
> Fond of fish-shaped Paumanok, where I was born—
>   fond of the sea-beach,
> From Mannahatta I send the poems of The States.

From this beginning spread the long poem we know as 'Starting from Paumanok', which began in Whitman's mind as the prelude to his third edition, the first of the great collections of *Leaves of Grass*, sometime between January and May of 1856, and was set down on paper beginning in the notebook drafts of October 1856.

This evidence supports a letter of 21 June 1856 in which he wrote of his determination to concentrate on the *Leaves* and on no other book. I should place this letter after what I have called the vision of the great new *Leaves of Grass*.

The Barrett manuscripts contain other evidence. In the manuscript version of the poem 'To One a Century Hence' that may just possibly have been written on his birthday on 31 May, he speaks of himself as thirty-eight years old in the eighty-first year of The States. This dates the poem in 1857, a fact not previously known since he altered the references in the final copy for the 1860 edition to read forty years old and the eighty-third year of The States, dates that wrongly make the poem appear to have been written in 1859.

Other references also centre on the year 1857. In June of 1857 Whitman wrote on a scrap of paper: 'The Great Construction of the New Bible. Not to be diverted from the principal object—the main life work—the three hundred and sixty five.—It ought to be ready in 1859.' This sets the target year for the publication of the third edition as 1859. On the other hand, only a month later he seems to have changed his mind. In a very important letter dated 20 July 1857 Whitman wrote as follows:

I wish now to bring out a third edition—I have now a hundred poems ready (the last edition had thirty-two.)—and shall endeavor to make an arrangement with some publisher here to take the plates and make the additions needed, and so bring out the third edition. In the forthcoming volume I shall have, as I said, a hundred poems, and no other matter but poems— (no letter to or from Emerson—no notices or anything of that sort)—It is, I know well enough, that THAT must be the true Leaves of Grass—and I think it has an aspect of completeness and makes its case clearer.—The old poems are all retained. —The difference is in the new character given to the mass, by the additions.

What seems to have happened is this. In June of 1857 Whitman is planning a third edition of *Leaves of Grass* that will comprise 365 poems, a project he hopes to have ready two years later in 1859. But the next month, apparently recognising the utopian nature of this project, he is willing to settle for the immediate publication of a third edition consisting of one hundred poems. The first thirty-two poems will be printed from the stereotype plates of the second edition, and thereupon will follow sixty-eight poems never before printed, all of which are already composed.

Let us pause now and turn to the manuscripts. Among them is a leaf containing a rejected poem, and on its back is a list of numbered poems, the list starting with number 33 and continuing to number 72, at which point the list must have continued on another leaf, but this is lost. When we compare this list and its titles with various of the manuscript poems, we find, with some few omissions, a complete concordance of number and of title. And from the manuscripts we can continue the list, with only a few gaps up to 100 and then on to 102. Surely it is obvious that this list comprises the plan for one hundred poems in July of 1857, and that the numbering and the arrangement were very likely performed between June and July of that year. More important, it demonstrates beyond the shadow of a doubt that these manuscripts which are so numbered and titled must date before 20 July 1857, and must have been written and then copied out between the date of the notebook for 'Premonition' in October of 1856, and the end of July 1857. At one swoop we may do what has not been done before—we may date about fifty-five specific new poems of the 1860 edition as composed and copied in their preserved manuscript form in late 1856 and the first half of 1857.

Can we do better? It is speculation, but *if* the poem I mentioned which might have been written on Whitman's birthday on 31 May, but is surely to be dated in 1857, if this poem appears in its chronological order, the fact that it is numbered 101 with a question mark might even indicate that the one hundred poems for the proposed edition were written before the end of May. If this is so, at least one of the layers of revision that can be seen in most of the poems ought to date from between June and July of 1857 when Whitman altered his mind and began, as he thought, to prepare his third edition of one hundred poems for the press.

But can we do better still? Perhaps something more can be surmised. When we look at all these Barrett manuscripts, we see that the poems are written on four kinds of paper. By far the most numerous are leaves of a porous thin pink paper that has been identified as remainders of the wrappers of the first edition. Next in quantity are leaves of white wove paper. Then we have some leaves with poems written on the back of printed real-estate tax blanks for the City of Williamsburgh, which had been incorporated with Brooklyn in 1855, and a few leaves and slips of blue writing paper. What is immediately striking is that with only one or two explainable exceptions, all the numbered poems that had appeared in Whitman's list of July 1857 are written on the pink paper, as is the list itself, although some poems appear with revisions on the backs of the tax blanks. It is clear, therefore, that the pink-paper poems are the earliest, and that most, if not all, of the poems written on this paper date before July of 1857.

This pink paper is rather curious, for its irregular outlines show that it has been cut into leaves from the larger sheets that made up the book wrappers. The obvious thing for any investigator to do was to play jigsaw puzzles. First, all the leaves with identical contours were piled together, and then the process began of fitting together a leaf from each of these piles to reconstruct the original whole wrapper sheet. It soon became clear that Whitman had stacked full sheets of the wrappers on top of each other and had then cut the pile

into six separate packs of leaves. From the Barrett manuscripts I found ninety-seven leaves out of a possible hundred
and twenty that could be fitted together to reconstruct one
such pile of twenty full wrapper sheets cut into leaves, and
parts of two other piles of full sheets could also be reconstructed. Then it became clear that by noting the occurrence
of the six different sets of leaves from the one fully constructed sheet, one could show that the leaves from each
pack of twenty similar leaves were inscribed before Whitman
turned to another pack. Moreover, it was possible to show
the order in which he used each of these separate packs, and
this order corresponded with the natural sequence one
would get from cutting up the pile of wrapper sheets in
normal progression.

Starting with 'Premonition', therefore, which was not
only the first-designed poem of the 1860 edition but also the
first inscribed, one can place the majority of the poems on
pink paper in a precise order of writing—on the physical
evidence of the leaves of paper and their matching contours.
Another kind of evidence joins to this. Whitman's day did
not know the blessings of paper clips; and hence he used
common pins to attach batches of leaves together. He
pinned these leaves together in the centre, usually, and each
time he unpinned a batch to make an addition or to look the
leaves over for revision, he made new holes when he pinned
the papers together again. These pinholes thus form recognisable patterns that can themselves be matched to
supplement the evidence provided by the paper and to show
what leaves were pinned together at one time. By corre-
lating all the evidence, the critic now can tell the precise
order of inscription of a large number of these poems.

The physical evidence of the manuscripts, and the external evidence of Whitman's letter, thus join to set a date of mid-1857 for the pink-paper poems. But why was a third edition not published in 1857, as planned, and what about the poems on the other papers? Some time in February of 1857 Whitman became editor of the newspaper the *Brooklyn Daily Times*. I should be willing to guess that one reason why he changed his mind between June and July of 1857 and decided to issue one hundred poems rather than wait until 1859 to write 365 was that he found the newspaper was taking more and more of his energies. And if poem 101 is really a birthday poem in late May, I should not be surprised if the majority of the sixty-eight new poems had not been written before April, perhaps even before March, of 1857. If so, it was a great spurt of poetic energy to produce this large body of verse between October of 1856 and March or April of 1857.

It seems evident that Whitman did not find a publisher in 1857 for his third edition. A business depression was beginning and was to grow increasingly severe as the year advanced. As late as June of 1859 it appears that Whitman was still in financial difficulties despite his regular job as editor for the two preceding years. Obviously, Whitman found no publisher willing to take the risk, and he could not finance an edition from his own pocket. There is every reason to believe that from the summer of 1857 to the summer of 1859, in late June or early July, when Whitman gave up his editorship, his whole energies were devoted to his newspaper work and that he wrote scarcely a line of verse for these two years until the end of his tenure came in sight, in March of 1859, and he began another spurt of poetic energy that was to equal the original one that had produced the sixty-eight to seventy pink-paper poems in the winter of 1856–7. This is the evidence of the paper.

The next sure date we have in the manuscripts comes in the poems on white paper. Here we find that the draft for what was to become Calamus, no. 2 was inscribed on the back of a discarded editorial about the Brooklyn waterworks that must have been written a day or two earlier than 15 March 1859. Now we can start matching up evidence from poems written on the backs of discarded drafts of other verses. Thus in a Whitman notebook dated 26 June 1859 we find drafts for lines 'Comrades! I am the bard of Democracy', lines that are early versions of a later draft that was discarded and its back used to compose white-paper Enfans d'Adam, no. 5. This intermediate draft of the 'Comrades' lines was in turn revised and finally appears on blue wove paper as part of the major expansion on white and on blue paper that was given 'Premonition'—on the evidence of the papers—after June of 1859.

That lines dated in late June of 1859 were still to be twice revised before reaching their final form and position brings us to the latest date we can be sure of. What we find is that poems on pink paper can be dated only in 1857. Correspondingly, poems on white and on blue wove paper can be dated only in 1859, and the earliest of these comes in March. It would seem that after a two-year interval Whitman, near the end of his newspaper job, began to compose furiously again. In all, twenty-six poems were written on white paper in the spring and doubtless the early summer of 1859, and a major revision was given to the earlier pink-paper poems, including a very considerable expansion of the long poem 'Premonition', all before the unknown date sometime in the summer or early autumn of 1859 when Whitman bundled up his manuscripts and sent them off to Rome Brothers. That he continued to write is shown by the twenty-seven additional poems composed after this point but before the copy was sent to Thayer and Eldridge. That Rome Brothers' proof was returned to him and that he was revising it in 1859, before 1 January 1860, we can tell from the change made in poem 101, in which—in proof—he altered his age from thirty-eight to forty, and the year mentioned from 1857 to 1859.

Now it is time to try to make something out of these facts and to apply the dates to a critical study of the growth of the *Leaves* of 1860.

To my mind, the point of chief interest centres on the changes in Whitman's plans as reflected in the dynamic growth of the structure of the whole volume. The key to the 1860 edition is its arrangement into what Whitman called 'clusters', that is, sections composed of poems written on a single theme. Thus the 1860 volume began with 'Proto-Leaf', the printed form of the manuscript 'Premonition', followed by the early 'Song of Myself' now retitled 'Walt Whitman', this followed by a section called 'Chants Democratic', then 'Leaves of Grass', then 'Enfans d'Adam', followed by 'Calamus', and then miscellaneous poems under 'Messenger Leaves', and finally just assorted poems without formal division. This third is the only edition with all these clusters. In the next, the process began of breaking them up and redistributing the poems.

The interesting point about the new cluster arrangement

in the 1860 edition is that the idea came to Whitman very late indeed. I suppose if critics have thought about it, they have imagined that all the new poems put into the clusters were written with the cluster principle in mind. If so, they must have been somewhat puzzled about the significance of some of the placings, for the pertinence of various of the poems in their particular clusters is not always very clear. The answer is, of course, that on the evidence of Whitman's 1857 list and the numbering of the manuscripts on pink paper the textual critic can assure the literary critic that in Whitman's original plans for a third edition he had quite a different order in mind and one that bore no relation whatever to the cluster principle. Close study of the early arrangement may reveal its rationale, but at the moment this is not to be solved by inspection.

Of the Chants Democratic cluster, and others except for Calamus, there is no trace whatever in the manuscripts. Thus one can guarantee that with the exception of any of the last twenty-seven poems written too late to be sent to Rome Brothers for proof, no poem placed in Enfans d'Adam, in Chants Democratic, Leaves, or Messenger Leaves, was written with these clusters in mind. This is not to say, however, that once Whitman decided on these clusters he merely inserted poems in just the form in which they had been written. One of the more fruitful sources of literary study in these manuscripts is to trace the changes made in proof, from the final manuscript version, in the interests of welding various independent poems into their assigned clusters. As one small illustration, we may take a few instances from Chants Democratic, no. 4, the poem called 'Feuillage', in manuscript, a long patriotic poem about

American life and different American scenes. This poem catalogued most of the regions of the country, it chanted the immensity and growth of America in statistical and some-times rather 'unpoetic' verses; and it included most of the vocations and labours of American men and women. Once Whitman conceived the Chants Democratic cluster, he set out to emphasise the theme through every technique at his disposal. The added lines, not present in the manuscript, usually bear on the unity of the country—lines like the addition, 'Always these compact lands—lands tied at the hips with the belt stringing the huge oval lakes'. Or—'All These States, compact,—Every square mile of These States, without excepting a particle—you also—me also'. In this last are compressed all the basic themes of Chants Demo-cratic: all-inclusiveness, wide range, America, and the personal address.

At another level, the expansion of a verse by the addition of a catalogue was intended to emphasise the nationalistic approach of the cluster. In the manuscript he had written, 'The city wharf—the departing ship, and the sailors heaving at the capstan'. In the proof this was expanded to 'The city-wharf—Boston, Philadelphia, Baltimore, Charleston, New Orleans, San Francisco, | The departing ships, when the sailors heave at the capstan'. By this roll-call of great American ports in their clockwise order, and the universa-lising of one ship to all the ships leaving all these ports, Whitman worked out a theme of greater scope and signi-ficance. Incidentally, while on the subject of Whitman's lists —the manuscripts show that he revised these in composi-tion as much as if not more than any other parts of his poems. These lists meant something to him, rhythmically, in sound, but more especially in their selection; and no student can afford to ignore them. They represent Whitman the conscious artist as much as any other feature of his verse, whether or not he knew that he was in the tradition of patriotic poets who have always exalted the names of their homelands.

Another interesting insertion is the line, shortly after this about the departing ships, 'O lands! all so dear to me—what you are, (whatever it is,) I become a part of that, whatever it is'. This emotion-charged verse reflects the poet's response to democratic America—'the land so dear to me'—and thus renders personal the theme of the poem. Also, it serves as a transition from the preceding verse, which ends with the words 'my lands', to the succeeding verses in which the theme of unity is carried forward by Whitman's identifying himself with the non-human elements that combine to form the background of human life in America. Indeed, through this added verse (and especially through the words 'I become a part of you, whatever it is'), Whitman prepared the reader for the daring conception of himself as one of a flock of great birds, 'I screaming, with wings slow flapping', and so on through other extraordinary metamorphoses—

I with the spring waters laughing and skipping and running. ...I, with parties of snowy herons wading in the wet to seek worms and aquatic plants; | Retreating, triumphantly twittering, the king-bird, from piercing the crow with its bill, for amusement—And I triumphantly twittering....In Kanadian forests, the moose, large as an ox, cornered by the hunters....And I, plunging at the hunters, cornered and desperate....And I too of the Mannahatta, singing thereof—and no less in myself than the whole of the Mannahatta in itself, | Singing the song of

These, my ever united lands—my body no more inevitably united, part to part, and made one identity, any more than my lands are inevitably united and made ONE IDENTITY.... Cities, labors, death, animals, products, good and evil—these me.

There are a few significant deletions. Although Whitman prided himself on including evil as well as good, he wished no outright evil practice or weakness in democracy to be celebrated in his Democratic Chants. For example, in the 'Feuillage' manuscript he had written, 'A slave approaching sulkily—he wears an iron necklace and prong—he has raw sores on his shoulders', and again, 'The runaway, steering his course by the north star—the pack of negro-dogs chained in couples pursuing'. These verses had an effective quality of definiteness and concreteness found in Whitman at his descriptive best, but for the sake of the cluster he sacrifices them as not suitable for exposition along with the greatness and wonder of American Democracy. Similarly, later in the manuscript we read, 'In the low dance-cellar at night the bloat-faced prostitutes drinking at the bar with the men', and this picture of the riverman's life along the Ohio was excised.

The one cluster that we know from the manuscripts was forming in his mind in the spring of 1859 was the Calamus group, devoted to manly love, or comradeship. Of all the manuscripts, the biographer and critic will seize on these for their relation to certain vexed questions in Whitman's biography. Very briefly, this is what the manuscripts tell us. Although homo-erotic imagery is not absent from the 1857 poems on pink paper, and although there are a few rather mild comradeship poems, the theme is by no means stressed, and it plays a comparatively small part in the hundred original poems. On the other hand, almost every poem on the white paper, dated in 1859, is in some way or another concerned with what has come to be almost a fixation with Whitman. The most obvious example comes in the extensive 1859 white-paper additions to the 1856–7 poem 'Premonition'.

There is much to be said for the theory that as a poem this 'Premonition' is the key to our understanding of the third edition. Throughout its manuscript history every alteration and addition that was made to this long poem was reflected in the general poems of the 1860 text. This is not strange, of course, for 'Premonition' was supposed to be the announcement or proem to the edition, the place in which the themes were stated and the basic ideas set forth. So it is that 'Premonition', like the third edition, grew slowly in Whitman's mind. Many glimpses into this process of growth and modification can be recovered as we see Whitman writing in additions and insertions, and cutting, pasting, inserting, deleting, and reassembling the leaves.

It is evident that the themes for the third edition, as shown by the pink-paper 1857 manuscripts, and by the original notebook and then the 1857 form of 'Premonition', —it is evident that these themes were essentially the same as those emphasised in the 1855 and 1856 editions of *Leaves of Grass*; and this is not surprising once we know that the earliest form of the poem goes back to late 1856, and that the basic third edition was prepared in completed shape as early as July of 1857. These original themes were: (1) the personal —as represented by the opening lines, but with no direct reference to comradeship; (2) democracy—as represented by the sections on 'These States' and on equality; and (3) religion—as represented by emphasis on the unity of the material and the spiritual, and on the fact of immortality, even though in a Whitmanesque sense. All of these themes in 'Premonition' and in the appropriate poems of 1857 were, from the beginning, meant to be treated—and indeed were treated—in a tone of exuberant optimism, and confidence.

As Whitman developed as a poet and thinker, we can follow in these manuscripts the development, in parallel, of his themes. Verses emphasising more definitely the poet's role as prophet were among the earliest insertions; and greater space was given to religion and to tradition, in line with this theme. But most important of all, almost certainly (one would think) as the result of some unknown experience, the theme of comradeship, the Calamus theme, becomes a major one in the additions to 'Premonition' as well as in the other poems of the third edition; and the result is a curious bifurcation of theme and effect. The disharmony is partly felt in 'Premonition' even though the theme, in the additions, is usually treated with the exuberance of the rest of the poem. But this confidence and optimism is seldom felt in the Calamus section of over forty poems that was to follow. And though Whitman did his best to unify this theme by endeavouring to universalise comradeship as part of his general democratic emotion and love of all humanity, ordinarily the experience was too personal and private in its expression for this treatment to be successful, and in some few poems it is quite clear that Whitman sees it even as in direct conflict with his function as poet-prophet and as the singer of songs for America.

The Calamus poems in 1860 are really out of place—especially as a cluster—since they are essentially a collection of love poems, the only ones that Whitman ever wrote.

As such, they bulk larger in the New Bible than they can merit in the total pattern of Whitman's poetic national thought; and they represent the intrusion of his strong private emotions upon his literary art in a manner that he was not at this time able or willing to control, although later he did so. Indeed, the chief problem presented by the Calamus poems lies in two factors: (1) their very theme; and (2) their unusual power and moving force. Whitman's early admirers considered these poems on a generalised and objective level as presenting something like the concept of idealised comradeship treated in English Renaissance literature. But this concept was not Whitman's, and the tenderness, the sense of shame and personal anguish that appear almost everywhere in the Calamus cluster rule out such an interpretation and enforce the belief that these poems spring from a serious private disillusionment.

Among the white-paper manuscripts from the Calamus section are twelve particular poems, widely scattered in the 1860 print, but originally written as part of a little notebook that can be put together again leaf by leaf through the details of its paper, a notebook that contained only these twelve poems and a few blank leaves. This little sequence has a title, what might almost be called a cluster-title, 'Live Oak with Moss', and from the first two of these poems it is clear that Whitman is using the live-oak and its companion moss as a symbol of male comradeship. All these twelve poems are fair copies, scarcely revised. Together they tell a connected little story of attraction, joy, desertion, despair, and sublimation. I am far from sure that at the start Whitman intended ever to publish them. At any rate, these twelve poems are the original beginning of the whole

Calamus cluster and its theme. The strongly thematic white-paper poem, part of Calamus, no. 2, written on the back of a rejected editorial of about 15 March 1859, has a number before it. Although the number duplicates the number of an earlier poem on pink paper, this white-paper poem seems to have been intended originally for a *Leaves of Grass* arrangement before the cluster idea was originated as the moving principle for the third edition.

We come to this sequence, thus. At the very start Whitman fixes on the symbol of live-oak and moss in a series of private poems, poems of the sort he calls sonnets. One or more homo-erotic poems celebrating the calamus, a variety of sweet flag or water-lily, were written subsequently (about mid-March 1859) and before a cluster was in mind as a focus for third-edition poems. At some later time and just before the manuscripts were sent to Rome Brothers, Whitman broke up his little personal notebook of twelve poems, crossed out its title 'Live Oak with Moss', and in the last of the inks he used in his revisions substituted the heading 'Calamus-Leaves'. I take this definitely to indicate the title of the cluster. In addition, Whitman wrote on another piece of paper an introduction to the calamus poem on the back of the editorial, and—in the same ink as the introduction—an extension, in another poem that became Calamus, no. 4, in which he specifically exchanges the live-oak symbol for the calamus, which he announces 'shall be the special token of comrades—this calamus-root shall, | Interchange it, youths, with each other—Let none render it back'. At the end he returns to the theme, 'But that I drew from the pond-side, that I reserve, | I will give of it but only to those comrades who love as I myself am capable of loving'.

It has been known ever since 1921 when Emory Holloway saw these manuscripts and reprinted the manuscript text of one poem, that the short poem beginning 'Once I passed through a populous city', a poem that in print is addressed to a woman, in manuscript celebrated a comradeship experience with a man. This poem, in some respects the most intimate Whitman wrote on the theme, perhaps because of its precision of reference and its intimate detail, was shifted in the 1860 edition with a change of sex to the procreative sequence Enfans d'Adam, intended to balance the Calamus cluster but doing so rather weakly, and padded with a few poems that have no connection whatever with the subject.

The key poem of this Enfans d'Adam sequence is the first set of verses in the cluster, 'To the garden, the world, anew ascending', in which Adam—as part of a cyclic resurrection —speaks. However, the major heterosexual references that in the printed text make this the theme-poem for the cluster were added in proof after the final form of the manuscript. Moreover, the manuscript, though it has no title, was given what seems to be a section-heading, 'Leaves-Droppings'. This phrase had been used in the second edition of 1856 to head a general miscellaneous section; and its application here seems to indicate, first, that when these manuscripts were sent to Rome Brothers a balancing cluster to Calamus had not been planned; and, secondly, the Adam title for the heterosexual cluster, as it was eventually put together rather arbitrarily out of earlier poems plus a few directly written for the group, probably came almost by accident from this single poem about Adam written under different circumstances and with no procreative or heterosexual purpose whatever.

When in the Calamus sequence Whitman wrote, in no. 44 near the end, 'Here my last words, and the most baffling,' and (again) 'Here I shade down and hide my thoughts—I do not expose them, | And yet they expose me more than all my other poems', he was surely opening the door to a personal interpretation of this cluster as actively tying in with his life and thoughts. For those who wish to venture on difficult reconstructions of a poet's mind there is much material in these manuscript versions, not only in the revisions in which one can see a personal theme developing and sharpening, but also in those that tone down a too great frankness (as against a few that increase the shock content deliberately), all this combined with the important added layer of revision that took place in proof between the final manuscript and the printed form.

I leave this subject without regret to indicate one or two of the more interesting kinds of revision from a more abstract literary point of view found in these manuscripts. That Whitman was almost always successful in these manuscript revisions is a tribute to his conscious artistry and to his ability to shape his poems more than has been supposed was possible for him. This is a good example of the way he worked. In the Feinberg notebook containing drafts for 'Premonition', we have these trials:

> Filled with such wonders
> How splendid the sun!
> Underfoot the
> O divine soil!
> Underfoot, O divine soil
> Overhead O
> How curious, how real
> Underfoot the divine soil!

> Overhead the sun!
> How curious
> How curious I myself

These fragments reveal Whitman testing his phrases, almost certainly by ear, attempting to adjust them to the precisely desired form. After various other attempts (including 'How curious is the brown real earth! | How curious, how spiritual is the water') these jottings become:

> How real is the ground! Come let us set our feet upon
>   the ground;
> How perfect and beautiful are the animals!
> How much room, and splendor! How inevitable!
> How spacious!

But this expansion, he sees, is getting him off on the wrong track; he reverts to his original ideas, and we get:

> Life—how curious, how real,
> Space and time how filled with wonders!
> To walk, to breathe, how delicious.
> The day! the animals! identity! eyesight!
> Underfoot, the divine soil,
> Overhead, the sun.

Somewhat later this becomes:

> This then is life, and this the earth.—
> How curious! How real!
> Underfoot, the divine soil,—overhead, the sun.

And finally he arrives at the complete form:

> This then is life,
> Here is what has risen on the earth after so many
>   throes and convulsions.
> How curious! How real!
> Under-foot, the divine soil—overhead, the sun.

Throughout the manuscripts Whitman was concerned to secure vividness and precision and to avoid the triteness of the usual poetic language of his day. For example, in the poem 'France, the 18th Year of These States', he first wrote rather slackly, 'I did not despair so much—I did not weep so much'. With a vehemence that makes the original reading hard to decipher, Whitman disgustedly crossed out this line and wrote, in marked contrast, 'I was not so deadly sick from the blood running in the gutters—nor from the single corpses, nor those in heaps, nor those borne away in the tumbrils'. All this vividness grew out of 'I did not despair so much—I did not weep so much'. This is the Whitman we admire for vitality and boldness.

It is especially interesting to follow him through half-a-dozen attempts to end the last poem in the 1860 volume, 'So Long!' This is not the place to trace all the ramifications of the changes made in the different drafts (at one time six revision slips were pasted one on top of another). But a few examples of the development may be quoted. The earliest ending went, 'Do not forget me—I must depart— | I love you—but I launch myself from you and from all that live, | I am as one who has done with materials'. This became, 'Do not forget me—I must depart— | Remember my words —I progress on—I expire from materials, | I am as one disembodied'. This slackness after several more tries grows tighter and more concentrated, and Whitman finds the right cadence, the inevitable series, for his triumphant close. 'Remember my words—' he writes, 'I love you—I depart from materials, | I am as one disembodied, triumphant, dead'.

This 'So Long!' is in fact an extraordinary poem, a more

successful summing up of Whitman's beliefs and aims than any other in the 1860 edition, perhaps. And it is singularly characteristic in the curious use he makes of erotic imagery for non-erotic statement. The final section of the poem, in which Whitman is saying farewell to the reader of this third edition of the *Leaves*, uses the symbol of death to describe the conclusion of the reading and the end of the reader's attachment to Whitman as the last page is turned. It was part of Whitman's prophetic vision that he felt himself to be his book, and his book to be himself. Hence as the reader is fingering the last pages and bidding farewell to the poet, Whitman thinks of the relation of author and reader summed up in sexual imagery as the epitome of the closeness that has come to exist between the two. And the held book becomes Whitman in the flesh. The conclusion of reading becomes the final act of love, of greatest intimacy, and this merges into the death imagery as Whitman departs, unconfined by the reader's experience and what part of himself he has shared goes on into a life for Whitman which, for the reader closing the book, is a parting as of death.

> What is there more that I lag and pause? That I
>   crouch extended with unshut mouth?
> Is there a single final farewell?
>
> My songs cease—I abandon them,
> From behind the screen where I lay hid I advance
>   personally.—
>
> This is no book,
> Who touches this touches a man,
> (Is it night? Are we here alone?)
> It is I you hold, and who holds you,
> I spring from the pages—decease calls me forth.

O how your fingers drowse me!
Your breath falls around me like dew,
Your pulse lulls the tympans of my ears,
I feel immerged from head to foot,
Delicious—Enough.—

Enough, O deed impromptu and secret!
Enough, O gliding present! Enough, O summed-up
    past!

Dear friend, whoever you are, here, take this
    kiss—I give it especially to you,
Do not forget me—I feel like one who has done
    his work, I progress on,
The unknown sphere, more real than I dreamed,
    more direct, darts awakening rays about me,
Remember my words—I love you—I depart from
    materials,
I am as one disembodied, triumphant, dead.—

THE NEW TEXTUAL CRITICISM
OF SHAKESPEARE

I HAVE suggested that problems present themselves to the biblio-textual critic in three main categories: the analysis of an extant manuscript; the recovery of the characteristics of a lost manuscript; and the analysis of authority in the history of textual transmission.

With the possible exception of some lines in *Sir Thomas More* of which the status is in doubt, no manuscript by Shakespeare has come down to us. Hence Shakespearean textual criticism must concern itself exclusively with problems of recovery and of transmission. I do not intend any implication that the textual critic of Shakespeare can be indifferent to those manuscripts of contemporary plays that have been preserved, and to their characteristics, for these will serve as the basis for hypotheses about the forms of the lost Shakespearean papers. All I mean is that, wanting any certain example of Shakespearean manuscript material, the critic has nothing tangible to analyse.

We must always keep one thing firmly in mind. Ultimately, textual inquiry comes to rest on the authentication of every individual word in every Shakespeare play as—on the available evidence—what we may believe to be the very word written by Shakespeare. On the available evidence, most of the individual words can be so authenticated. Other individual words seem to any common-sense literate view manifestly either wrong or else to be such errors as to constitute no words at all. These are clearly in need of emendation. A third range of individual words has evoked suspicion. Some editors are inclined to emend; others, not. The case is in doubt, more or less legitimately, depending upon the particular circumstance. In most of these questions the original reading makes some sense, and the temptation to emend is in direct proportion to the difficulty with which the original may be defended, weighed against the attractiveness of the proposed alteration. There is a fourth range, words which to most editors have seemed to be authenticated but which miscellaneous persons (usually of little textual or critical experience) suggest should be emended. The columns of *Notes & Queries* and occasionally the communications to *The Times Literary Supplement* are quarries for such suggestions to alter the text of Shakespeare in respect of quite satisfactory words.

To be complete we should add a fifth range that cuts across and includes these four but adds fresh complications. When a Shakespearean text is preserved in more than one version with some claim to authority, the problem of authenticating the individual words grows more serious. If we set aside the independent problem whether variant readings represent the original and its authoritative Shakespeare revision, we find difficulty enough in assessing which variant is the true reading and which a corruption resulting from the process of transmission. Although the odds certainly favour the superiority of readings in a generally more authoritative text, for any given individual word the inferior text's variant may prove to be the authentic reading, in one's editorial judgement. No text is so poor, not even the bad quarto of *The Merry Wives of Windsor* or the bad first quarto of *Hamlet*, but editors have commonly agreed in preferring at least a few of its variant readings. And when texts approach nearer each other in authority, as in Q2 and Folio *Hamlet*, or in Q and F *Othello*, the balance between variants becomes much more delicate.

When we inquire what agent decides to which range we may assign the individual words of Shakespeare's text, just about the only answer is *critical judgement* or *common sense*. No linguistic or bibliographical argument has any operative validity until the results of its application are accepted by the critical judgement. Moreover, critical judgement means the judgement of more than one man—ultimately what we can only say is common consent. Of course, we must not require common consent to include every ultimate consumer of a text: we need not secure the assent of every teacher in every school before agreeing that a reading is acceptable. We may take it that common consent embraces chiefly those critics and editors whose opinion is powerful enough eventually to shape the form of the edited texts that penetrate to the schools. These might be as many as fifty scholars. They might well be fewer, perhaps considerably fewer.

This selective opinion is likely to be conservative. In the United States, at least, it has ordinarily rejected John Dover Wilson's and C. J. Sisson's texts of the Complete Works, though both advance new bibliographical or palaeographical methods as the reason for their being. In single-volume editions it has not taken seriously as other than school texts such ventures as the New Arden, the New Yale, or the Pelican editions, for example. It has, generally, hewn to the Old Cambridge (or Globe) text, and to Kittredge or to Peter Alexander. Clearly, in England or in America no new authority has arisen since the 1860's that can be said to have the force of a definitive approach to the text producing results that have secured general acceptance such as that given to the Old Cambridge in its day and since. Perhaps the Oxford old-spelling edition now under way again after the lapse following the death of McKerrow will become the new authority, but there are no present means for estimating the prestige that will accrue to it.

This is not to say that in many directions we have not made admirable advances in the application of modern scholarship, both linguistic and bibliographical, to the problems of Shakespeare's text. We have, indeed; and a number of quite encouraging practical gains have been secured. On the other hand, as yet no one scholar has 'spread-eagled' the field and, by his own research and his assimilation of the research of others, has acquired such a total view and such a synthesis of present-day knowledge as to establish general acceptance of his text in the manner that was possible for the chief editor of the Old Cambridge edition.

It may be that the task is too great, the amount of theory and information too extensive, for the intellectual effort of synthesis to be made and a text defined. I do not really think so, however, although we must not underestimate the difficulty for any single individual to have, and keep in balance, the necessary linguistic, bibliographical, and purely critical abilities that will be required. Nor is the committee system the answer.

However, I should say that we are not properly ready for anything but provisional results. Using both bibliographical and linguistic approaches, we have been able to chip away at the huge problems, and various positive results have been achieved. But we lack much more basic information than we have yet won, despite the astonishing renaissance of Shakespearean textual scholarship after the Second World War; and until this dark area is better illuminated we shall be in no position to think of synthesis. Something of the nature of this withheld information, and the methods by which it is at present being attacked through bibliography, are the subject of this discourse.

One of the prime fallacies still prevalent among Shakespeare's editors is the attempt to solve the problem of authenticating or of emending the individual word in Shakespeare's text without first reaching a working general hypothesis about the nature of the manuscript of which this word was a single part, or counterpart, and the physical circumstances by which this manuscript was transferred to print. Some such mechanical base to use as a continual reference for the implications of the critical judgement is a necessity, especially with texts for which multiple authority is preserved.

In our post-war attempts to exhaust the possibilities of what may be called scientific, or mechanical evidence before offering the results for critical decision, we must be particularly careful not to be misled by the pseudo-scientific or the pseudo-bibliographical. A case in point is offered by the old-fashioned palaeographical school recently and somewhat anachronistically revived. In his recent studies of the Shakespearean text, Mr Sisson argues that he has in various cases recovered the correct Shakespearean reading by writing out in Elizabethan script the faulty word as it was printed, and seeing what other word might be suggested by its appearance. In theory this other, suggested, word is the lost Shakespearean original that was confused by the compositor.

On some occasions, unquestionably, this writing-out may serve as a powerful stimulus to the creative imagination that is so frequently the source of an inspired emendation like 'a babbled of green fields'. Moreover in cases where there has been simple confusion it serves to limit the area of conjecture. It will not assist with the problem of whether in *Romeo and Juliet* a rose will smell as sweet by another 'name' or 'word'; but in *Macbeth* it offers some reasonable physical grounds for the critical preference for 'tune' rather than 'time' (4. 3. 235).

Nevertheless, underlying this method are at least three potential false assumptions that cause difficulty when it is extended too far.[1] First, its tacit assumption that all corruption is caused by misreading ignores the known facts of memorial error by a compositor, so frequently demonstrated in reprints. Thus if a critic prefers Romeo's 'Then I defy you, stars' from the bad Q1 instead of *deny* from the good Q2, a memorial lapse, but not a misreading, must be posited. In a review of Sisson, Professor Shaaber remarks on the excesses of the palaeographical method: 'Once in a while, in fact, it becomes almost an obsession. Speaking of "On, on, you Noblish English" (*Henry V*, III. I. 17), an example of attraction if I ever saw one, he says, "There can be no reasonable doubt that *noblest* was in the original copy misread as *Noblish*" (II. 61).'[2] By reducing the whole wide field of compositorial error, as here, to a single narrow explanation, the palaeographical school ignores the evidence for textual corruption discovered by modern bibliography.

Secondly, the reversibility of palaeographical evidence is assumed, a proposition against which Sir Walter Greg, a very great palaeographer himself, has quite rightly protested. For instance, an Elizabethan *a* without the horizontal stroke across the top, or a well-defined diagonal to close the letter, might easily be confused with a *u*; but a *u* is much less likely to be misprinted as an *a*, for in that case quite different assumptions would be required. The way in which letter formations hit the eye, also, are not always reversible. For instance, Sisson plumps for *solid flesh* in *Hamlet* and— ignoring all the important bibliographical evidence—hinges his case on the probability (as he takes it) that *s-o-l-l-i-d* was misread as *sallied*. I must say, to misread a very rare word indeed like *sallied* as *sollid* would not in my view be at all impossible; but for this Q2 compositor to misread a common simple word and in the process somehow to arrive by chance at the peculiar word remembered by the Q1 actor-reporter and the word used later by Polonius only in the good text (and set by a different compositor) is to argue what seems to be the impossible. When arguments from handwriting can be carried to this length to rationalise a choice of readings, or to the length where it is seriously suggested that the compositor of *Hamlet* misread *tunes* as *lauds*, it is time to call a halt.

Thirdly, the palaeographical method of textual criticism requires the assumption that there was something approaching a normal Elizabethan script and that the modern critic's own version of this script would therefore be virtually identical with the appearance of the word in whatever diverse manuscript was used by the printer. I take it that this assumption is most seriously suspect because handwriting differs so markedly between individuals as in large part to negate much specific similarity of letter formation and thus of similar ambiguity in two hands. If a compositor misreads a word because one or more of its letters are malformed, to suppose that the malformation might also be probable, or possible, in a dozen different handwritings is to strain credulity. That my own capital *T* is often mistaken for a *C* or a *J* does not mean that this will be a common error in all hands. Some errors are natural, and common, such as the difficulty of distinguishing *im* and *un* in the Secretary hand, for instance, and the ordinary confusion between Secretary *e* and *o*; but by and large the script was by no means so uniform that we may be justified in assuming that the letters a compositor might misread in Sisson's script are those he might misread in Shakespeare's or in any of the various scribes who also provided printer's copy of Shakespearean texts.

Indeed, the case goes beyond the simple one of diversity of letter formation in Secretary hand. To varying degrees Italian letters were interspersed in Secretary forms, not always in a consistent manner. For example, in the manuscript of the play *The Welsh Embassador* in the 1620's sometimes a Secretary *e* is used, sometimes a Greek ϵ. An initial *c* may be written in either of two different forms, at random, both manifestly intended to be minuscules, although one is, in fact, the majuscule form. Other letter forms are not always stable. If this play had been printed and the manuscript lost, palaeographical emendation on the assumption that all *e*'s were Secretary would often be quite wrong; nor could correct arguments be invariably adduced based on the assumption that initial minuscule *c* was conventionally in the minuscule Secretary form.

Hence to attempt to emend Shakespeare's printed texts on the tacit assumption of a uniform Elizabethan script without regard for the fact that the printers' manuscripts for Shakespeare's plays must have been in the hands of a variety of scribes, as well as some in Shakespeare's autograph, is to use a theoretically scientific method in a suspiciously unscientific manner. I have yet to find a 'handwriting' critic who distinguished one jot between his suggestions for emending the text of *The Merry Wives of Windsor*, say, and the text of the Second Quarto of *Hamlet*, although the manuscript for the one must have been in the hand of Ralph Crane, of which we have a number of examples, and the other is supposed to be in Shakespeare's autograph, for which we may have part of *Sir Thomas More*, or we may have only signatures.

The modern insistence on first attempting to discover the nature of the manuscript before approaching the authentication or the emendation of the individual words of a text has much wider implications, however, than simply to help clarify the use of palaeographical evidence. Most textual critics prefer to work with a naïve transcript of an original rather than a sophisticated transcript. The reason is not far to seek: presumably it is easier to recover true readings from ignorant errors than from a smoothed-out transcript in which the presence of error may be impossible to detect. For example, when in the Folio Hamlet says 'Oh good Horatio' (5. 2. 355), we should scarcely suspect the phrase of error were it not for the Second-Quarto reading

'Oh god Horatio' backed by the First Quarto's 'Oh fie Horatio' which together show the Folio reading to be a sophistication, though many editors illogically still prefer 'good'. Similarly, a textual critic who can hypothesize an authorial inscription under his printed text has only one layer of transcription, the compositor, to peel off before recovering the author's original; but a critic who must hypothesize a scribal transcript under his printed copy must peel off two layers of transcription, scribe *and* compositor. In this case, of course, the normal inference is that, all other things being equal, more corruption will be present in a text that stems from two or more transcriptions than from one. Hence, one would expect the textual critic to emend a text printed from a scribal transcript more freely than one printed from autograph, simple correction aside.

Ordinarily this expectation is gratified, but not always; and when the opposite is true, then the hypothesis should be scanned very closely to see why editorial practice has not followed editorial hypothesis. For instance, consider the text of *The Merchant of Venice*, which in general is quite clean and not much in need of emendation; and compare it with the text of *Hamlet* in the Second Quarto, which is usually thought to be far from clean and much in need of emendation. Formerly, both quartos were thought to be printed from Shakespeare's foul papers, and the numerous difficulties of *Hamlet* were blamed on the printer. But recently the identification of the compositors has demonstrated that the same two workmen set both plays, and hence that printing-house conditions cannot be blamed for the difference in result. Obviously we must take another look at the theory for the manuscript behind the *Merchant*, and it may be that future critics will decide on new evidence that it is a scribal transcript. If so, then editors had better examine the text more rigorously than before, in search of hidden corruption, or else face the seeming paradox that a quarto (*Hamlet*) typeset by the same two men from what seem to be Shakespeare's papers is more replete with error, not all of it naïve, than the quarto set by these men from a transcript.

But let us revert to the opening propositions—that the Shakespearean textual critic and bibliographer concerns himself chiefly with the twin problems of recovery and of transmission. Actually, the problem of transmission is only an extension of the basic problem of recovery, and there is no essential difference between them except for the degree of complexity that they represent. For our purposes, however, let us define the problem of recovery as the attempt to identify in the printed text as many characteristics as possible of the lost manuscript; and, correspondingly, to identify in the print the characteristics of the printing-house when these differ from the manuscript. The latter is an essential process, since manuscript characteristics can be isolated only after the printing-house characteristics have been recognised. Many non-bibliographical critics have confused the two, such very different scholars as Dover Wilson and Helge Kökeritz, for example, commonly taking it without investigation that repeated anomalies are authorial rather than compositorial.

The attempts to define the nature of the manuscripts behind the printed Shakespearean editions has been only loosely bibliographical in the past. Sir Walter Greg, who pioneered the attack on this problem—as on so many others

—has been the most active investigator; but he has chiefly used the analysis of stage-directions as his evidence, combining this material with occasional suggestions from the variation of speech-prefixes, and bringing up the rear with some analysis of the kind of error in the play, as seemingly coming from a manuscript difficult to read, or one causing no difficulty. Valuable as this method has been, it is approximate at best, and the only really meaningful division that can be attempted is that between theatrical and non-theatrical manuscripts; or, sometimes a non-theatrical manuscript with some theatrical annotation. Moreover, as the newer bibliography based on compositor-identification begins to move in on the problem, some of Greg's theories about these manuscripts are being more and more seriously questioned, on evidence that is concrete and less subject to personal interpretation or chance. A case in point is what we can now infer about *The Merchant of Venice* manuscript (or about that of *Hamlet*) by comparing *The Merchant* with Q2 *Hamlet*, once we know the precise pages in each set by the same two compositors. Moreover, this same study has served as a useful criterion against which to measure non-bibliographical hypotheses. John Russell Brown's analysis of the two compositors in James Roberts's printing-house has indicated that various spellings in the quarto *Hamlet* that Dover Wilson had isolated as authentically Shakespeare's own are in fact merely compositorial.[1]

The new research that will eventually provide us with the answers we require derives completely from compositor-identification and analysis. It has long been known that compositors could be identified by their individual spelling proclivities, like the *A* and the *B* compositors of Shakespeare's First Folio. But, principally because it has still had an insufficient factual basis, this knowledge has scarcely been used until now, except for some pioneering work by Alice Walker and the late Philip Williams. For example, Dr Walker theorised that compositor B was more prone to sophisticate a text than the more conservative A. This will ultimately turn out to be quite true, I think; but the evidence will need to be re-studied in some part because at the time of the investigation no one was aware of the existence of the apprentice compositor E, later so brilliantly identified by Charlton Hinman. Hence in all studies of compositor B to date, the bad work of E has been attributed to B, and the waters correspondingly muddied. It is of particular interest that Dr Hinman's researches, when fully published in the future, will identify on irrefutable evidence the work of all the Folio compositors, even to the part-column, and will for the first time add a pair of compositors C and D whose work on the Comedies section has either been confused with A's or else lumped together as an unknown quantity X.

One difficulty with spelling-tests is that they are ordinarily not so exact as to deal with units of less than a page, and sometimes even whole quarto pages may easily be in legitimate doubt. But Dr Hinman is now able to identify First Folio compositors with absolute precision, not only by spelling-tests and presswork probabilities inferred from the order of running-titles and box-rules in their repetitive use, but also by tracing the exact use of types, out of identified cases, from typesetting to distribution to typesetting again, and so on through the different cases that were used by the Folio workmen. This analysis results from the positive identification of hundreds and hundreds of slightly damaged types so that, in mass, they can be traced through the pages—the individual course of each of these hundreds of types can be plotted as they are set, distributed, find their way, with or without their fellows, into specific cases and are again and again used to set certain pages after each distribution.[1]

When the detailed results are published and we have all the five Folio compositors precisely identified, and when similar studies are made for each substantive Shakespearean quarto, we can then proceed to two applications. First, by a study of these compositors as they set other books we can estimate their incidence of error and thus make assumptions about the amount of emendation that will be required. Moreover, analysis of the kind of error found in the work of the different compositors who set Shakespeare's texts will undoubtedly give us factual bases, now wanting, for the kind of emendation required according as we find certain compositors responsible for certain pages of the text.

Allied bibliographical studies will be of assistance. For example, hard on the heels of Hinman's brilliant discovery that the First Folio was set and printed by formes, generally from the inside of the quire out, instead of the pages being composed in seriatim order, other studies have established a wholly unsuspected amount of setting and printing by formes in Elizabethan dramatic quartos.[2] The application of this new information about Elizabethan printing techniques has already produced results.

Not so long ago G. B. Harrison argued most persuasively that in such late plays as *Antony and Cleopatra* and *Coriolanus*, Shakespeare was inclined to break a regular pentameter line into two irregular lines as a rhetorical device to secure the rhythm and emphasis that he wanted to hear when they were recited.[1] And Harrison had a little quiet fun with the editors who followed Pope's regularising of these broken lines and thus smoothed-out Shakespeare's indicated intentions. Although no voice was raised at the time, critics should have known better than to accept these arguments, for common sense would inquire how an actor could possibly recall such minutiae when his memory was loaded with the large number of plays required by Elizabethan repertory conditions, even if the scribe who copied the part from which the actor memorised his lines had followed such indications from the Shakespearean original, or from the scribal prompt copy or intermediate transcription. But we need no longer trust to such objections, pertinent as they are, for Hinman has shown conclusively that what the literary critic exalted as Shakespeare's subtle art was in the main only a compositorial device to waste space in circumstances when the cast-off copy was insufficient to fill the page with normal typesetting. So much for critical theory as against what bibliographical fact can demonstrate.

On the other hand, when the cast-off copy for the forme was too great to fit into the space assigned, the compositor was reduced to various expedients to save room, such as running verse lines together, omitting all interlinear white space, and even—as Hinman has some evidence—excising some of the text in cases of emergency. These are newly discovered and most significant pieces of evidence about the effect of the printing process on the text. But the end is not in sight. For example, if we can explain various anomalies in a text as being the result of the casting-off of copy and the typesetting by formes, we are helping to restore the shape of the original manuscript as we strip away some of the veil of print. Occasionally the results can be most important. For instance, whenever we may assign verse set as prose, or prose as verse, to a precise mechanical cause, and not to the characteristics of the underlying manuscript, we can save ourselves from false assumptions of some consequence.

The second method of compositorial study will be slowly and painfully to analyse the characteristics of those workmen who set Shakespeare's substantive texts, so that in some degree we shall be able to identify the influence of the manuscript copy on the printed result. That is, although compositors had their favourite ways of spelling some words, and sometimes an invariable way, their practice was not uniform and was often susceptible to influence from the spelling, capitalisation, and perhaps the punctuation of the copy. We may study these characteristics against control texts, chiefly when these compositors were setting reprints, and in this manner discover what spellings are their favourites and what spellings are indifferent. Then we shall have something approaching a scientific basis of factual evidence to assess the influence of the manuscript and to recover certain of its characteristics as filtered through the compositorial treatment.

At present only an occasional and uncertain light can be thrown on the subject by presupposing what it is dangerous to presuppose, that notably eccentric spellings derive from the manuscript and not from the compositor. We have seen how misleading this method was when applied to the quarto *Hamlet* without bibliographical safeguards. Certainly, the opportunity that Dr Alice Walker most ingeniously seized on in *Romeo and Juliet*[1] does not present itself every day. She observed that the Second Quarto had the misprint *c-h-a-p-e-l-s* for the word *chapless*, or, 'without lips'. She then pointed out that the compositor of this quarto (actually two compositors, as we now know) was an *-esse* speller and therefore the reading *c-h-a-p-e-l-s* was not a simple transpositional error by this compositor trying to spell *chaples* (for he would have set the form *chaplesse*) but instead a true mistaking of the manuscript; that is, the compositor must have thought that the word was in fact *chapels*. The nature of the misreading, therefore, as set against the compositor's known spelling habit, successfully demonstrates that in the manuscript the word *chapless* was spelled *-les*. If the manuscript is a Shakespearean autograph, as there is some reason to believe, Dr Walker has recovered an authentic Shakespeare spelling. This is very good indeed, but obviously such evidence is not found very often.

To return to the spelling evidence—once we build up a body of bibliographically confirmed information about the spelling characteristics of the various manuscripts behind Shakespeare's plays, it is not too much to hope that marked similarities and dissimilarities may become clear between texts, and that slowly we may construct a basis of fact that we can use to identify a Shakespearean manuscript by the non-compositorial spelling characteristics of the printed text, or else that we may do something towards distinguishing the hands of certain scribes that may reveal themselves as alpha, beta, gamma, and so on. The late Philip Williams made a most ingenious start in this direction.[2] In the text of *1 Henry VI* he observed that the name *Joan* in the First

Folio is sometimes spelled *Joane* and sometimes *Jone*. However, which—if either—is the manuscript spelling is in
doubt since the distinction is purely compositorial: the
Joane forms all appear in pages set by compositor *A*, the
simple *Jone* forms all in pages set by compositor *B*.

However, in this same play he also observed that scene
division did not begin until Act 3, although compositor *A*,
who had set Acts 1 and 2 without division, would scarcely
be likely by himself to start division when he also came to
set Act 3. This difference between division and no division
is emphasised by certain spelling differences that exist in
the same copy set by compositor *A*; thus in Acts 1 and 2
Burgundy is spelt invariably with a *d* as *Burgundy*; but in
Act 3, corresponding to the introduction of scene division,
compositor *A* changed and thereafter invariably spelled the
name *Burgonie*. Equally striking is the designation of Joan of
Arc as *Puzel* eighteen times in Act 1, but *Pucell* twenty-six
times in Act 3, all in pages set by this same compositor *A*.
Williams drew the inevitable conclusions: the printer's copy
for this play was heterogeneous. This in itself is information
of especial interest bearing on the authority of the text in its
two sections. Moreover, it may be that in the future one or
other of the two hands could prove to be Shakespeare's
autograph. Whether this or not, the good possibility exists
for making a start here with some basic observations about
manuscript characteristics in Shakespearean texts. And in
this connection it may be suggested that though the compositorial spelling *Joane* or *Jone* was of no value in determining that the copy was heterogeneous, it might have some
value if one or other form were shown to be uncharacteristic
of the compositor concerned and could thus be inferred as

a copy spelling, provided the other spelling was correspondingly shown to be characteristic of the workman who
used it in this text.

Williams also observed that in the Folio the variant
spellings of the ejaculation 'Oh' as *Oh* or simple *O* seemed
to be consistent in one or other form in some plays regardless
of the fact that more than one compositor set the texts; and
from this evidence he conjectured that the spelling might
be useful as one characteristic to aid in distinguishing the
hands of the manuscripts. Moreover, in a play like *King
John* when the spellings switch from simple *O* in the first
three acts to the predominant *Oh* form in the last two acts,
Williams felt that this fact could justifiably be added to
other significant evidence to suggest that the underlying
manuscript was not uniformly the work of only one inscriber.

Williams carried forward such evidence very boldly to
suggest that *Coriolanus* and even *Timon of Athens* were not
printed from foul papers, as Greg supposed, but instead
from scribal transcripts; and I may say that Dr Hinman on
other evidence will partially confirm Williams' views about
Timon of Athens when his monograph on the First Folio
is published.

Casting about in the First Folio, Dr Williams further
noticed that in *Titus Andronicus* the Fly Scene (added in
manuscript to the quarto copy that served the printer otherwise) exhibits some differences in spelling that cannot be
compositorial, as for instance the spelling of *vppon* with two
p's, a rare circumstance in the Folio; or the spelling of
Tamora's name with an *i* as *Tamira*; or the change in speech-
prefix from *Titus* to *Andronicus*. These all constitute significant evidence that manuscript characteristics can indeed

show through the veil of print. Finally, to conclude such evidence, Williams pointed out that it might be the case that compositor *A*'s spelling of *to the* as *toth'* in *Macbeth* and *Coriolanus*, but nowhere else in the Folio, linked these manuscripts beneath the print; and that it would not seem to be chance that *A*'s work in *Henry VIII* and in *Hamlet*, in his opinion, is linked by a phenomenally greater use of semicolons than was *A*'s custom, a link supported by the aberrant spelling *wee'l* in both texts.

The validity of such evidence as this in other dramatists than Shakespeare has been demonstrated, but much other evidence remains in Shakespearean texts. For example, as one of several ranges of evidence in an investigation into the relation of Q2 to Q1 *Hamlet*, I found that the identified Q2 compositor *X* in setting the second quarto of *Titus Andronicus* from the first had in general added somewhat to the heaviness of the punctuation; but if Q1 *Hamlet* had been annotated to serve as printer's copy for Act 1 of Q2, as has been asserted, then he behaved in quite the contrary manner. In his share of *Titus*, compositor *X* added eighteen commas while omitting eight; but in *Hamlet* he would have added only fourteen as against omitting seventy-five. Other punctuation evidence also pointed in opposite directions between the two typesettings. Moreover, certain exceptions in *Hamlet* to invariable spellings found in *Titus* and in *The Merchant of Venice*, in *X*'s pages, seemed to refer to manuscript since they were not reproductions of Q1 spellings at such points. The view that Act 1 of *Hamlet* in Q2 was set from manuscript instead of from annotated Q1 seems to me to be certain, on the evidence;[1] and on the evidence a few of the manuscript spellings can be identified to add to the small store that—greatly increased—will one day settle whether this, or other plays, was set from a Shakespeare autograph or from a scribal transcript.

The problem of transmission is essentially that of recovery, but greatly complicated. In a play like *The Merry Wives of Windsor* the recovery of the characteristics of the manuscript as they show through the print indicates that the identifiable scribe Ralph Crane wrote out the manuscript that was the printer's copy. The nature of the manuscript that he used in turn as *his* copy is obscure. Very likely few of its characteristics can be ascertained by compositor study since Crane usually seems to overlay what he transcribes from (although this matter has not in fact been scrupulously studied in various Crane texts by treating him as if he were a compositor); and one would expect the Folio compositor to further the process. However, here as elsewhere with less strong-minded scribes than Crane, at least in theory some small pieces of evidence might be dredged up to enable us to speculate from something other than wishful thinking about the earlier copy.

As an example of new evidence about transmission and the occasional role that recovery of a manuscript may play in such an investigation, one may cite *Romeo and Juliet*. The conventional theory has been that the good second quarto was set up from Shakespeare's foul papers, except for one passage that was substituted (probably for a lost manuscript leaf) from the bad first quarto, without annotation. Some occasional consultation of Q1 elsewhere has generally been allowed in places where the compositor might have been troubled by illegibility. But recently Professor Dover Wilson has advanced the theory that considerable portions of the second quarto were typeset from annotated leaves of the bad first quarto.

What is the truth, and how may it be made manifest? Going about the task bibliographically, the way it should be done, Dr George Williams has arrived at some important conclusions.[1] First, he determined that two compositors set the good second quarto, and he identified their pages. He then studied the habits of these two workmen in setting various contemporary plays from printed copy and tabulated the individual characteristics that appeared in their transmission of printed text. When these identified characteristics were applied to Q2 of *Romeo and Juliet*, the marked variation between the work of these compositors in the quarto and their work when transmitting a printed document gave evidence that a manuscript did indeed underlie the whole of the second quarto except for the familiar leaf of Q1. Thus Professor Wilson's non-bibliographical assumptions were shown to be mistaken.

However, more important results appeared from this careful bibliographical investigation. The highly variable speech-prefixes of this quarto, as between *Wife*, *Mother*, *Lady* for Lady Capulet, have always been taken as classic examples of McKerrow's suggestion that such variation ought to indicate the presence of an author's foul papers, since a composing author might well have written from the point of view of the character's function in the scene, as for example whether Capulet were in relation to Juliet, in which case he might be *Father*; or in a formal capacity, in which case he might be *Capulet*. But tempting as this theory has seemed, it has never entirely held water, since if the pattern of personal relationships were scrupulously carried out, Capulet would end by being 'father' to his wife, and also to his daughter's nurse, a proposition that is nowhere encouraged by the play.

Dr George Williams observed, however, that some sort of pattern could be developed on other than assumed literary grounds. For example, the regular prefixes for Capulet up to Act 3, scene 1, are *Capu*; but with Act 3, scene 4, when this form appears it is shortened to *Ca* except for 4. 2, and 5. 3, in which *Cap*, *Capu*, and *Capel* also occur. Beginning with Act 3, scene 5, the *Ca* prefix is irregularly replaced by the functional *Father* prefix. So, in general, with the variant forms for Lady Capulet. Coincidental with the start of Act 3, scene 5, on signature H2 verso, when this break in the pattern starts and the speech-prefix *Father* is introduced, a marked increase in the capitalisation appears. In sheets A to G between thirty and fifty capitals are used per eight pages; but starting with 3. 5, sheets H to M use from sixty to ninety capitals. The increase, starting at 3. 5, is marked and is in vivid contrast to the practice in 3. 4. For instance, in dialogue the terms *father* and *mother* appear in lower case from 1. 1 to 3. 4; but these words of address are capitalised from 3. 5 onwards. Other changes in these later sheets from gathering H can be seen, such as a general tendency to capitalise the start of a clause after a question mark, as against the earlier preference for lower case.

Now the importance of the compositorial analysis becomes clear, because these characteristics of the later sheets are found in the work of both compositors and cannot be assigned to any bibliographical division or unit. Hence it is clear that what we have is a reflection of some difference between the early and late parts of the underlying manuscript and thus this manuscript cannot be the homogeneous foul papers previously supposed. In the further investigation, once again compositorial analysis becomes important. According to Dr Williams's views, although these speech-prefix and capitalisation differences can be clearly seen occurring in the work of the first compositor who bridges the two sections of the manuscript, other variants do not appear, at least in so far as he has analysed the text to date. Hence his present opinion, on evidence that may not be quite exhaustive, is that both sections of the manuscript are in the hand of the same writer; but that the section from 3. 5 to the end represents an earlier and rougher form of the manuscript, and the first section an authorial fair copy. Whether this provisional hypothesis will stand up to closer investigation I do not know, but its promise is high; and in the end the scholarly inquiry into the transmission turned up valuable information from the recovery of manuscript characteristics once the red herring of Q1 copy, conjectured by Dover Wilson, was shown to be a red herring.

This investigation into the transmission of *Romeo and Juliet* ended in establishing the authority of a single text (except for whatever extremely limited authority may be allowed the memorially-reconstructed bad first quarto). But when the study of the transmission establishes double authority in separate editions, very serious difficulty may ensue. The difficulty is certainly more acute for such texts as *Hamlet* and *Othello*, and possibly *Troilus and Cressida*, than it is when the second authority is weaker, as for plays like *2 Henry VI*, *The Merry Wives of Windsor*, *Romeo and Juliet*, *Henry V*, and *King Lear*, in which the second authority is a bad quarto. Nevertheless, in all these cases the characteristics of the manuscripts of both editions must be recovered as closely as possible, and the precise relationship of the two editions in the matter of the transmission of the text must be established.

The central problem of the Shakespeare double texts is the relationship, and therefore the transmission. Are they printed from independent manuscripts? Is the later printed from a copy of the earlier edition that has been annotated with corrections and revisions from some manuscript? Was the printer's copy for the later edition some combination of the two? These are questions of the utmost importance. For some of these plays critics had thought the answer was settled; but the trend of recent investigation, rightly or wrongly, has been to cast doubt on most of the conventional conclusions. It now seems quite possible that Folio *Henry V* was not set from an independent manuscript but instead from an annotated quarto, perhaps even sections of the two different editions, annotated. Only recently has Dover Wilson's own attempt to upset conventional opinion about *Romeo and Juliet* been controverted, and—for once—conventional belief upheld by strictly bibliographical evidence. The question of the exact quarto edition or editions that were annotated to form the Folio printer's copy for *Richard III* has only recently been decided in favour of Q 3 (1602). One investigator has even wondered whether in some part annotated leaves of the bad quarto were not used for the Folio printer's copy of *The Merry Wives of Windsor*, which would seem almost impossible.

The uncertainty about these plays is bad enough, but it is worse to be in complete doubt—as we are so far as real demonstration is concerned—about the relationship of the quarto and Folio texts of 2 *Henry IV*, of *Hamlet*, and possibly of *Othello*, texts not yet subjected to rigorous bibliographical investigation. These are, of course, transmission problems, and they concern transmission in two senses. First, whether the later text was set from an independent manuscript or whether a printed quarto was annotated by reference to such a manuscript, the problem is singularly important—what is the relation of these two lost manuscripts? Is one representative of autograph copy and the other of scribal transcript, as has been conjectured for *Hamlet*? Or—as may be possible for *Troilus and Cressida*—was the earlier quarto annotated for the Folio by reference to a manuscript in an earlier stage of composition than that behind the quarto?

This question may arise even in the bad-quarto texts. When Q1 of *Hamlet* agrees with the Folio against Q2 (supposed to be set from autograph), does this Q1 then preserve some of a revision, or else of theatrical alteration; or is Q2 merely corrupt in such readings? Is Dr Hosley right to alter the second-quarto text of *Romeo and Juliet* in order to stage a scene according to the first-quarto system of entrances, one that seems to represent the company's adaptation of staging that Shakespeare in the manuscript behind Q2 had carelessly left difficult if not impossible to produce as written? As Mr Cairncross has recently asserted in the New Arden edition, do some omissions and alterations in the Folio 2 *Henry VI* reflect censorship changes for a later production, and will the purer text at such points be found in the bad first quarto, as a consequence? Are some details of Q1 *King Lear* more authentic than the Folio text? In *Hamlet* is the Q1 position of the nunnery scene that of the stage version as against the 'literary' version of Q2, the Folio concurrence with Q2 being explained by the derivation of its print essentially from the Q2 print?

In some part the answers to such questions do not involve strict bibliographical investigation; but there can be no doubt that the second respect in which transmission problems exist does depend exclusively on bibliographical analysis—and that is the question of the physical relationship of any two texts, whether positive or negative. The importance of knowing the precise copy from which an authoritative text is typeset is crucial. For example, if Folio *Hamlet* were set from an independent manuscript, then concurrence of Q2 and F in a reading would be very hard to explain away, and we should need to appeal to theories which the odds do not favour, such as error in the autograph original faithfully copied by one compositor and one scribe; or the inscription in the original of a word in a manner that would quite independently be copied as the same error by these two agents. Thus if one believes that in *Hamlet* the reading *breathing like sanctified and pious bonds* found in both Q2 and Folio is wrong, and that Theobald's emendation of *bawds* (*bauds*) is correct, as I firmly do, then if Q2 and Folio came from independent manuscripts we should need to suppose that *bauds* was so written in Shakespeare's autograph that the compositor of Q2, and the hypothetical scribe who may have been employed to copy out the foul papers to make up the theatrical manuscript, both independently misread the *a* as an *o*, and the *u* as an *n*. This is possible, of course, but the probability decreases rapidly with each additional common error that must be so explained; and there are more of these common errors than are altogether comfortable for any advocate of the independent manuscript theory in its pure state. I am myself particularly interested in the apparent refinement in i. 5 by which in both texts Marcellus calls *Illo* but Hamlet *Hillo*. I cannot conceive that this is a meaningful distinction, and to my mind it suggests that Q1 *Ill, lo* has contaminated the text of Q2 and that the corruption has been passed on from Q2 to the Folio.

Thus if the Folio were set from annotated Q2, or if Q2 exercised a direct influence on Folio in some other manner, we should be required to accept a much simpler hypothesis: merely that in each case the annotator or scribe overlooked the error, and hence it was automatically passed on from quarto to Folio.

The logic is clear. If *Hamlet* Q2 and Folio derive from independent manuscripts, concurrence of the two texts in any reading would ordinarily be the guarantee of authenticity of every such word in which good cause for double error could not be found. (And there is a practical limit to the number of such double errors that a critic can accept under these conditions.) When the two texts differ, then the relative authority of the respective manuscripts must be balanced against the nature of the difference, so long as some coherent theory of choice is maintained and the process does not degenerate into mere literary eclecticism, without any underlying principle except tradition and personal taste.

On the other hand, if the Folio were typeset from an annotated Q2 or in some other manner came under the direct influence of the quarto, concurrence of two readings is no guarantee whatever of authenticity in any individual case. The paradox is plain that when two such texts differ, we can usually assume that the variant in the later was the result of a conscious annotation or alteration more often than it may be taken as a compositorial aberration, whether conscious or unconscious; thus it will ordinarily represent the reading of the manuscript that was being conflated with the print. Yet when two words agree, we can never be sure that the scribe did not simply skip over a difference and fail to notice that the word in the quarto did not represent the word that appeared in the manuscript.

Hence the relationship of the two texts in plays like *Hamlet*, or like *2 Henry IV* or *Othello* or *King Lear*, is no idle academic quibble, but a problem that must be solved before any editor can properly shape his own resultant text, or can even begin with such preliminaries as attempting to assess the nature of the manuscript that underlies the Folio print. It seems almost impossible to believe that when we know our compositors well enough, we cannot use our information about their habits when they transmit printed copy—such apparently trivial matters as the influence on these compositors of the spelling, punctuation, and capitalisation of printed copy—to settle the question once and for all and to demonstrate beyond all possible doubt the exact transmission of these debated texts. The case will rest either on positive or on negative evidence, depending upon the transmission or lack of transmission of hundreds and hundreds of minor characteristics. Taken alone, the evidence of substantive readings is often crude and indeed contradictory; and very often explanations can cast doubt on the validity of this evidence. Frequently such evidence will carry no conviction to a bibliographer trained to respect evidence that in the main is not susceptible to critical alteration by the human element engaged in the transmission. The more mechanically produced the evidence, and thus the less likely to be subject to conscious evaluation by the persons engaged in the act of transmission, the more scientifically based is the method of bibliographical investigation of the transmission process. Thus the concurrence or variance of hundreds and hundreds of small points of spelling, punctuation, and capitalisation according to recognisable patterns divorced from identified compositorial habits should combine with evidence from readings to establish the truth in bibliographical terms. It is long past time.

Up to the present most critics have been forced to rely on the rough evidence of readings alone, since not enough has been known about the compositors involved to say with any assurance that the pattern of the so-called 'accidentals' of texts was significant or non-significant. For example, when one tries to estimate just where the first quarto of *Romeo and Juliet* was consulted for a few of the readings of the second quarto, it is a question of how exact the pattern of coincidence must be before one can come close to the demonstration of specific influence. The usual appeals to probability have a hollow ring in arguments that this comma must have influenced that comma, and so on. The question is difficult enough at best without attempting a non-bibliographical solution when a critic has in fact no precise information about how closely the compositor concerned was likely to follow the minor characteristics of printed copy.

The treacherous nature of substantive readings alone, backed by mere guesses as supplementary evidence about what is the transmission of 'accidentals', is well illustrated by the *Richard III* problem. At first, on the evidence of readings, it was believed that Q6, annotated, was the printer's copy for the Folio; then it was believed that in the middle and at the end some unannotated leaves of Q3 were present in the copy; recently a New Zealand scholar has published a monograph in which he reverses the whole by arguing for Q3 as the sole copy throughout; in answer to him a Scottish investigator argues for the use of Q3 as main copy but certainly supplemented by Q6, and he then adds the complication that some parts of the copy must have been leaves from Q1.[1] When critics can disagree like this over what is— after all—physical evidence, something is wrong. In my view that something is unquestionably the method, the reliance on substantive readings in the investigation of complexly derived printer's copy instead of the scientific use of the evidence of accidentals controlled by compositor-analysis, which is the bibliographical way.

The recognition of the need to estimate the exact nature of the printer's copy and its authority, and to establish all facts of transmission from it, as a required prerequisite to editing, is a major plank in present-day textual theory. And the development of a method for determining complex transmission by means of compositor-analysis applied to the evidence of the accidentals of a text has undoubtedly provided one of the most valuable tools of modern biblio-textual research.

I do not mean to imply that the need for information about the nature of printer's copy was not acutely felt before the Second World War, for here as in so many other matters that trio of great English scholars—Pollard, McKerrow, and Greg—was in the forefront. What I do have in mind, however, is that lacking anything but an approximate method, critics could make little specific use of such information in the editing of a text, and hence any discussion of printer's copy was more likely to be thought of as a topic of general historical interest than as a means for precise application to decide problems in individual textual readings. It is impossible to think back to the almost inexplicable decisions about transmission made by the Old Cambridge editors for *King Lear* and *Richard III* without remarking that the complacent faith in the single powers of literary criticism as applied eclectically to the text has confirmed the vast majority of readers in their preference for these same faulty texts long after the theory of transmission on which the editorial policy was based has been reversed. No editor came forward to revise these particular texts in the Globe edition according to the newly perceived history of their transmission. Neither did the publishers see the necessity for commissioning a revision, and the various textbook editors who continued to base their copy on the Globe showed no awareness that a major textual upset had occurred that ought to have important consequences as applied to the choice of readings. When such insensitiveness to the major bases of Shakespearean text is shown, it is easy to recognise the lack of pressure on editors that would follow general discussions about more obscure points of transmission. Greg once remarked shrewdly that editors who took it that the Folio *2 Henry IV* was set from an independent manuscript nevertheless edited it in practice as if the copy had been an annotated quarto. This is not the only case in which editorial theory and practice have not been consistent. Although Dover Wilson reversed the usual esteem given to the Folio *Hamlet* and held up the Second Quarto as the superior authority, his choice of Folio readings over the quarto was substantially that of the Old Cambridge editors who felt strongly the superiority of the Folio. And within the last few years, in editing *Romeo and Juliet* various of his preferential readings from Q1 have been in complete contradiction to his hypothesis about the relation of the two quartos at these points.

It may be that this editorial indifference to the practical consequences of the history of the transmission of a text has developed through some obscure recognition that much of the reconstruction of the history has been hypothetical and tentative and therefore perhaps untrustworthy. Despite the attempts that have been made to solve the problems of the double-text plays, absolute demonstration has not been achieved in such test cases as *Hamlet* and perhaps *Othello*; and the disparity between the three separate theories currently advocated for *Richard III* has not invited editorial confidence, doubtless. Hence when the purported specialists have failed to agree, the editor who does not feel capable of independent judgement through his own research has seen no incentive to forsake the easy ways of old-fashioned eclecticism.

It must be admitted that most critics tackling the problem of transmission today are still using the evidence of substantive readings in no essentially different way than occurred to P. A. Daniel editing the Praetorius facsimiles about eighty years ago. The failure of this evidence to be decisive in complex cases has been amply demonstrated both in the past and in the present. And only a thin veneer of what is usually pseudo-bibliography separates the treatment of evidence by modern critics from that by Daniel.

In some sense it is understandable that the newer bibliographically based techniques have not made greater headway, since they require a trained bibliographer to administer them and to evaluate the results, and the number of bibliographers with experience in textual application is severely limited. When meaning is involved, as with substantive readings, any intelligent man feels capable of analysing concurrences and differences. But the analysis of the evidence of masses of largely mechanical and therefore substantially meaningless 'accidentals' seems hopeless if not impossible to the critic who has had little or no experience in this dark area. Thus there has been a general tendency to cling to the old-fashioned reliance on substantive readings as the only trustworthy evidence for tracing transmissional history.

Moreover, some critics have been sympathetic to the bibliographical approach and have made pioneer use of compositor-analysis as applied to textual problems, but generally this interest in compositorial habits has focused on evaluating the correctness of substantive readings and has neglected the application to accidentals as a method for demonstrating textual transmission. In some part this reluctance to forsake substantives for accidentals is a clinging to the old in the face of the new; but in some part it may have been caused by a fear that the determination of habitual or preferential spellings was not an accurate enough method to establish the stints of compositors. And the absolute precision required by the use of accidentals as evidence for delimiting complexly ordered printer's copy cannot always be secured without compositor-analysis. Occasionally this fear has been justified. In some difficult cases, like the second quarto of *Titus Andronicus*, the identity of the compositor of even a whole quarto page may be in legitimate doubt if only spelling evidence is used. Moreover, mistakes may be made as in the confusion of the regular compositor *B* in the Folio with the apprentice compositor *E*, only recently distinguished by Dr Hinman.

But the publication of Dr Hinman's monograph will shortly offer a precise account, even to the part column, of all the compositors concerned with the Folio, the new evidence for identification by the cases of type, as well as by spelling characteristics, now providing bibliographical demonstration for the most part of an incontrovertible nature. Thus since every major Shakespearean textual problem ends in the First Folio, the exact determination of its compositors will offer the necessary factual base for the forthcoming bibliographical attack on the problems of transmission. This attack will have two prongs. First, variations from the habitual in the work from manuscript of the identified compositors will be studied in the light of their known practices, and this will produce facts and not mere impressions about the underlying manuscripts behind the plays printed for the first time in the Folio. Secondly, by the use of control texts the habits of the compositors when setting from printed copy can be ascertained in respect to their treatment both of substantives and of accidentals. The known patterns of the influence of printed copy on their characteristic setting of accidentals can then be applied to debated texts to settle by a more scientific method (because on more mechanical evidence) the exact nature of the underlying printed (or, negatively, manuscript) copy utilised by Jaggard's workmen.

It may then be hoped that once the facts are established

editors will make proper use of material that is no longer subject to debate, and will recognise how practical in its application to the solution of textual problems is the knowledge of the details of the transmission of texts. Yet the principles and purposes of this new editorial scholarship still seem to be very much misunderstood; and it is far too common an assumption that the more 'scientific' or 'bibliographical' an editor is, the more he is an enemy of eclecticism, and that his secret ideal is to print a 'safe' text with none but simple corrective changes from some one of its extant printed forms. This is a confusion of the principles of modern textual bibliography with the 'best manuscript' fixation that Housman so tellingly satirised. That bibliography and its attempted scientific method promote the most deep-dyed conservatism is a profound misconception.

What exactly does *eclecticism* mean? *Choice* is the operative word: an eclectic editor is an editor who chooses between alternative readings. Here we are immediately in the presence of one of the basic confusions about the process. It was to prevent the unprincipled selection, on grounds of personal taste, of readings now from one and now from another document of some authority that Lachmann insisted on the study of transmission. This produced for each work considered a family tree of manuscripts which should in principle reveal the single most authoritative, or 'best' manuscript, whose text (under such a condition) must be rigorously followed except for simple correction, or emendation to bridge the gap back to the lost original. Any other procedure, under these circumstances, was branded as *eclectic*. Except when the family tree produced two or more manuscripts radiating from the lost archetype (a case that Lachmann felt called for recension to restore the lost archetype, and emendation to bridge the gap between this and what the author intended), the attempt of the most scientifically minded non-eclectic editors was to reduce all authority to unity and hence to create a situation in which no true alternative reading could theoretically exist outside the 'best' manuscript; thus preference for a reading in a lesser authority must be unprincipled, or *eclectic*.

Although A. E. Housman in the preface to his edition of Manilius pretty well demolished the misapplication of the theory of unity and the attempt at all costs to find a 'best' manuscript to follow in cases when no such phoenix existed, Germanic rigour still exerts enough of a spell to be encountered now and then quite out of its element in the textual criticism of printed books. Indeed, printed books must have their own rules distinct from manuscript study. Immediate derivation of editions can almost always be correctly assumed in textual bibliography whereas manuscripts in a direct descent can always be assumed to have lost intermediates. This difference has profound consequences and makes extremely dangerous any attempt to carry over postulates from manuscript study for exact application to printed books.

When we consider the special problems of print we find that the definition of eclecticism adopted in 'scientific' manuscript study is too narrow, and in the process of expansion and re-definition the word loses much of its fearsomeness. What is not generally recognised is that any bibliographical editor must perforce be eclectic (in a sense) if he is not to print a mere facsimile, or what I like to call a diplomatic reprint. That is, even if an editor resolved to follow exactly every word in, say, *Two Gentlemen of Verona*, but to modernise the text, he would be forced into 'eclecticism' in hundreds of different ways, some problematical. If he modernises all words like *murther* to *murder* is he not being eclectic in that he chooses to believe that differences in such spellings have no effect on pronunciation? Suppose he (quite correctly) modernises *murther*, should he then change *lanthorn* to *lantern*? His choice—if he modernises— will be eclectic. What is the exact syntax? Time and time again a Shakespearean speech will begin a sentence with an independent clause, then follow with a dependent, but then hitch on an independent, the clauses separated only by commas. Whether the dependent clause, in modernisation, should be associated as dependent on the first independent, or as inverted before the second independent, is often a difficult if not impossible question to decide; yet any editor modernising the punctuation (or I should maintain, even an old-spelling editor) must be eclectic when he chooses which way he thinks it is and indicates his choice to the modern reader by his re-punctuation.

If an editor makes a single emendation, in a general sense he has produced an eclectic text, for he has made a choice between alternative readings. What is commonly misunderstood is that eclecticism is not confined essentially to the choice between readings from more than one text. Any emendation introduced into a play that exists in only a single text will result in a kind of eclecticism if the rejected reading could yet be argued as making some sense. The source of an emendation has no bearing on the question of choice between two possibilities. In this broad sense any edition of

Shakespeare must by the very nature of the case always be eclectic unless it is a facsimile or a diplomatic reprint.

Where the bibliographical textual critic parts company with the unscientific critic is in his insistence that eclecticism—this general as well as the more specific kind of choice between authorities—must be governed in all respects by logical principles developed from ascertained facts. Thus when collation establishes that in editions after the first no new authority has entered, and each edition is merely a reprint of an earlier, it is clear and logical that no variant in a later edition can in any sense be authoritative. That some readings may correct errors in the first edition is to be expected, but no editor would draw a reading from the Shakespeare Fourth Folio, say, as in any possible sense more authoritative because of its origin than an emendation of his own. Thus *corrections* may be taken from later unauthoritative editions, but never anything that can be thought of as *revisions* nor any readings that may be thought of as superior in their own right because of their origin.

An editor who ignores this principle does so at his peril. For example, Professors Black and Shaaber devoted some thousands of hours to a scrupulous collation of the Shakespeare Second, Third, and Fourth Folios against the First. Their considered conclusion, after examining all the data, was that not one piece of evidence existed that was strong enough in combination with enough other pieces of evidence to allow us to believe that the later Folios were anything but reprints, somewhat edited, it is true, and growing steadily more corrupt, but in no case with fresh authority entering. Hence when in *1 Henry VI* Sisson remarks that the Second Folio supplies two words that 'are necessary to the sense and can hardly be merely editorial', Shaaber is justified in protesting, 'If we are to entertain the possibility that new readings in F 2 have some authority it will be a merry world indeed'. The two words may or may not be necessary. But if an editor accepts them, he must do so only on the basis that they are mere guesses in the Second Folio. (He will, of course, have first exhausted the possibility that they were copied in F 2 from a previously unknown press-variant state of the page in the First Folio, in which case the matter of their F 1 authority would need investigation.) To take these words confidently, as Sisson does, as though they have authority, is to be eclectic in a way that bibliography cannot tolerate. The distinction here is a matter of principle that may have wide effects. A bibliographical editor, provided some such words seem necessary, might well be eclectic and make an insertion. But if he preferred two others of his invention, he would be quite justified in selecting those instead of the readings from the Second Folio since they too can only be guesses, provided they are not derived from F 1 press variants. To choose the unauthoritative F 2 readings automatically, would be illogical eclecticism.

One cannot deny that the insistence of bibliography that logic should prevail when eclecticism is exercised, and that bibliographical probabilities must always be satisfied, does indeed usually promote conservatism, although as Dr Walker has shown with *Richard III* in the New Cambridge edition it may paradoxically encourage in some cases more eclecticism than would ordinarily be acceptable even to the non-scientific critic. Let us see what may be meant by this logic. At 1. 2. 198 of *Hamlet* some editors prefer the Q1 reading 'dead vast...of the night' to the Q2 and F 1 *wast* (i.e.

waste). But if the Q1 reading were to derive, as it must if it is correct, from the manuscript behind Q2, or that behind F1, or from some intermediate manuscript, one or other text must be corrupt but not both independently. If *vast* is correct, the only possible explanation for the Folio *wast* must be that the F1 reading was derived from the Q2 print. Thus if an editor believed that the Folio *Hamlet* was set from an independent manuscript used as printer's copy, he could not adopt *vast* as the correct reading.

Or we may take the example of Dover Wilson's editing of *Romeo and Juliet* in the New Cambridge edition. Professor Dover Wilson believes that a rather large number of pages of Q2 were set from an annotated copy of Q1. If this were true, logic would require whenever such a page comes along that any variant from Q1 must be an error on the part of the Q2 compositor failing to follow the Q1 copy, or else the variant must result from an annotation in Q1 drawn from the authoritative manuscript used for comparison. In the nature of the case, one would expect the compositor's errors in setting from printed copy to be relatively few, and hence that the majority of the numerous variants ought faithfully to represent the manuscript annotations. Yet time and time again, the New Cambridge text selects the Q1 reading instead of the Q2 variant in pages where Q2, by editorial hypothesis, was set from annotated Q1 copy. In fact, this edition selects the Q1 readings instead of the Q2 variants rather more often from some of these pages than from pages where it was conjectured that Q2 was set from manuscript. On the face of it, this is a quite illogical editorial procedure, and it represents a truly unprincipled eclecticism that cannot be justified by bibliographical probabilities, and certainly not by the terms of the editor's own hypothesis about the nature of the printer's copy.

The subject is very rich indeed, but it can be only touched on here and so must conclude with *Hamlet*. Professor Dover Wilson's pioneer and exciting monograph on *Hamlet* exalted the Second Quarto text as set from Shakespeare's autograph foul papers, and therefore as deserving of our confidence; whereas the Folio was at least a transcript of a transcript of these papers, and hence sophisticated and untrustworthy by reason of its transmission history. The rehabilitation of the Second Quarto led to one of the poorest editions of *Hamlet* ever published, the Craig and Parrott text, which clung stubbornly to the Second Quarto and rejected eclectic transfer of readings from the Folio whenever possible. At the time this edition was supposed to be very scientific indeed because its anti-eclectic refusal to admit some of the traditional Folio substitutes seemed to follow admirably from the editorial hypothesis. The only trouble was, this edition was based on several premises about the transmission of the texts that are now demonstrably false, and hence the very rigidity of its anti-eclecticism led it into error that was better avoided by the unscientific eclectic editors who chose between readings pretty much according to their own taste.

It is, indeed, possible to be too rigid. In the 'To be or not to be' soliloquy in Act 3, scene 1, Kittredge, like most editors, prefers Q2's *despis'd* love to F's *dispriz'd*; although in the next thirty-five lines, of seven variants he takes the Folio reading in six, including *pith* for Q2 *pitch and moment*. Since Kittredge in general assumes that the Folio readings are more authoritative than those of Q2, one would like to know his reasons for the delicate choice of *despis'd* rather than *dispriz'd* since in case of doubt his editorial practice elsewhere should have inclined him to the Folio reading. Yet it would be somewhat improper, perhaps, to accuse him of inconsistency as between *despis'd* and *dispriz'd* and *pitch* and *pith*. It is almost an axiom that variants so close together in letters and sound are much more likely to represent corruption in either text than actual revision in the later. Although it would be theoretically more consistent to argue for memorial failure or misreading by the same compositor for both, in fact the words are as susceptible of error in the Folio, given its assumed textual history, as in the quarto. An editor may well feel safer in treating conjectured error as consistently as possible by reliance on what appears to be the more authoritative text. But lacking a truly bibliographical analysis of both texts of *Hamlet*, we may too easily fall victim to circularity of reasoning. Our literary taste leads us to prefer one text on the whole to the other, and hence we consider the one we prefer to be the more authoritative. I would be the last to deny that this line of critical reasoning often works in practice despite its circularity; nevertheless, its basis is sufficiently suspect to lead a cautious editor to hesitate to apply such presumptive authority with absolute rigour to all disputed readings.

However, even in the present incomplete state of our knowledge some limits can be set. An editor can scarcely reject any reading in which Q1 and F *Hamlet* agree against Q2 without explaining how this oddity came about. If he thinks that the Folio was set from an independent manuscript, then he must have good reason to emend any reading in which

Q2 and F agree. He absolutely must make up his mind whether he believes that Shakespeare did or did not revise the text after the stage represented by the manuscript under the Q2 print. If he is not prepared to take it that there has been revision, even so minor as might occur in the course of making an autograph fair copy, then he must recognise that whenever he prefers the Folio reading he must logically assume that the Q2 compositor has made an error. If so, it is necessary to see whether these assumed errors in Q2 fall into any sort of pattern that is explicable,[1] and, if a pattern develops, whether it may not be reversible, and apply with equal or greater force to the Folio variants in these cases.

Thus a choice becomes something more than a flitting here and there between the texts depending upon one's personal preferences. On the other hand, if an editor takes it that there has been some revision in the form of the manuscript as represented by the Folio, it would, even so, be absurd to choose the Folio in all cases of variance. As with *pitch* and *pith*, or *despis'd* and *dispriz'd*, not all variants come under the head of revision. Moreover, there is demonstrable evidence that some readings in the Folio are sophistications. Hence an editor must in any circumstances be eclectic, since in double-text plays some corruption must be expected in each form, to say nothing of the possibility of revision that an editor must always endeavour to follow.

The difference lies in the fact that an editor's choices should be guided by principles and must logically conform to these principles. If in *Hamlet* an editor believes in revision, he must evolve some principles that will guide him in selecting from the Folio the readings he thinks are authoritative alterations while rejecting those he thinks are editorial or compositorial non-authoritative variants. He must be prepared to justify his choices. If, on the contrary, he believes that no fresh authority entered the *Hamlet* text between the manuscript behind Q2 and the manuscript that in one way or another was behind the Folio, he must evolve some principles for deciding between Folio corruption and Q2 verisimilitude, or Q2 corruption and Folio preservation of the authentic Shakespearean reading. He must be prepared to justify his choices. Whether common error in both documents originated in their pre-printing or in their printing transmission must be decided. As remarked above, if he believes in the independent manuscript theory for the Folio, he cannot justify his choice of *vast* from Q1 instead of *waste*. If he holds that *pitch* is a Q2 compositor's error but *dispriz'd* a Folio compositor's error, he must have evidence for his decision when the choice seems on meaning to be so indifferent.

What is as yet almost unexplored except for Dr Alice Walker's pioneering investigations[1] is the evidence about the characteristics of different identified compositors as it may be applied to the problem of eclectic editing. In the above I have with some deliberation been speaking in general terms of *the* Second Quarto and *the* Folio texts of *Hamlet* as if each were a uniform and homogeneous representation of its underlying printer's copy. But these texts were not so. Both from the presswork and from spelling analysis, aided by the typographical evidence that in the different cases the founts of italic differed slightly, we are now aware that two compositors, X and Y, set Q2, and we know the precise pages composed by each. Partly from spelling evidence but chiefly from Dr Hinman's remorselessly logical use of typographical evidence, we now know that the Folio *Hamlet* was set by three compositors, *A*, *B*, and *E*. Thus we cannot appeal to general probability or to evidence from miscellaneous pages in any attempt to decide whether it is more likely that the Second Quarto, assuming such and such kind of copy, would mistake *pith* for *pitch*, or *dispriz'd* for *despis'd*, than it is that the Folio, set from such and such copy, would be mistaken in its variants for these readings. Instead, the bibliographical editor of the future will collect his evidence only from the pages of these texts set by the compositors in question. Moreover, these identified workmen set other plays, and their characteristics elsewhere become a part of the total evidence that will assist an editor to balance the compositors' observed treatment of the printer's copy in the play under consideration against their observed characteristics in setting other copy. Under such controlled conditions compositor-analysis may be used not only to provide an estimate as to the nature of the printer's copy, and thus to add to our general knowledge about the transmission of a text; it may be used also to apply to specific problems of transmission as represented in the question whether specific readings faithfully transmit the underlying copy. Certainly, to take only one example, an editor will estimate the authority of Folio readings in *Hamlet* somewhat differently depending upon whether compositor *A*, or *B*, or the apprentice *E* set the type.

In this way a knowledge of the printing process and an intimate acquaintance with the habits of specific compositors act as a constant check and balance on unbridled assumption. This is basic. But over and above such assistance one also has operative bibliographical principles about the relationship of texts that establish certain criteria to limit the area for eclectic procedure, and in this limitations often act as positive guides. The establishment of biblio-textual principles may act on some occasions to curb eclectic processes; but on others these same principles may act as a positive spur to encourage eclecticism. It is an ignorant view, and a positive misconception, that bibliography acts as a blue-nosed and puritanical censor to take all the joy out of the textual critic's life.

What, then, is the final purpose of this new textual method? Perhaps the most widely held opinion may be represented by the following from an eminent critic's review of Sisson's *New Readings in Shakespeare*. After commenting on Sisson's eclectic treatment of the *Hamlet* text he adds:

I will not debate the justifiability of this procedure. One might simply say that Mr Sisson is an unusually candid editor, for the truth is that no text of Shakespeare published since 1623, facsimiles alone excepted, is anything but eclectic. The nearest thing to a non-eclectic edition, the First Folio edition of the Misses Porter and Clarke, which blindly follows F, is one of the worst. The great twentieth-century enterprise of determining the rationale of the texts has had important effects, but still nobody has so far produced a non-eclectic text of a single play. What is more, I do not expect to live to see anything else, not simply because of the conservatism of publishers but also because of the inherent difficulties of the problem and the deficiencies of our knowledge of the printed editions on which we depend.[1]

To my mind this represents a too limited interpretation of the relation of bibliography to the editorial process and to the results that may be expected to accrue in the future. If we anticipate something that textual bibliography has no intention of giving us, we may not appreciate in correct terms what in the future we shall be offered.

If I interpret the statement correctly, the major contribution of twentieth-century textual method is considered to be the investigation of the nature of the lost manuscripts behind Shakespeare's plays for the specific purpose of determining in scientific terms which is the more authoritative manuscript behind any double text. Thereupon, the editor should ideally devote himself to the correction of that text *in its own terms* without eclectic conflation from any document printed from a generally less authoritative manuscript. This I take it is supposed to be the ideal non-eclectic text from which we are withheld only by the difficulties of the problem and the deficiencies of our knowledge of the effect of the printing process on the lost manuscript.

It will be clear that the argument of this present discourse is in opposition to such a view. It can no more be held for Shakespeare than for Manilius that in questions of multiple authority, any single manuscript—if we could only recover it completely and accurately from the print—would provide us with full information about what Shakespeare actually wrote. This is to assume that the printer's copy was invariably a Shakespeare holograph, an assumption contrary to fact. Even when the printer's copy was itself a manuscript, in some cases the exact recovery of this manuscript in every detail would give us only, as with *The Merry Wives of Windsor*, what a scribe copied and not necessarily from a holograph. But in what may well prove to be the commoner cases, those in which an earlier quarto was conflated with a manuscript to provide Folio printer's copy, recovery of the exact form of this annotated copy would not solve all textual problems. This particular kind of lost manuscript can never be recovered beyond the annotations transferred from it to the quarto, and on the evidence these were usually incomplete. Hence if *sanctified bawds* and *god kissing carrion* are right, proof that they are what Shakespeare wrote would not be found if the lost printer's copy for Folio *Hamlet* were discovered tomorrow and it proved to be an annotated quarto.

Whether a line may be drawn between the correction of a text in terms of its own rationale and an eclectic editing method is difficult to see. A 'scientific' editor might feel that he was not being eclectic if in *Richard III* he substituted in his basic Folio text all Q1 readings that had been passed on to the Folio in corrupted form from Q3. But the difference between simple correction of error and eclectic substitution is obscure, and not to be bounded by distinguishing mere mechanical error (like simple transposition, or assumed foul case) from corruption due to misreading or memorial error. Nor may non-sense in the selected text always call for what may be regarded as simple correction. In *Hamlet* 3. 1. 119 *euocutat* in Q2 may be admirably corrected by F *innoculate*; but would *pith* from the Folio be a demonstrable correction of Q2's *pitch*, or an eclectic substitution? And what of Q2 *despis'd* for Folio *dispriz'd*?

More serious trouble is encountered if (assuming Folio *Hamlet* as the chosen text) one were forced to keep *Oh good Horatio* from F at 5. 1. 355 instead of Q2's *Oh god Horatio*; or at 3. 1. 97 Folio's *I know right well you did* for Q2's *You know right well you did* on the grounds that it would be eclectic to adopt the Q2 readings. And perhaps even more difficulty would be caused by switching authority to Q2

and refusing to conflate from F. In *Hamlet* as in other plays
—even to leave aside the question of revision—no single
text among multiple authorities preserves in a state susceptible
of recovery from its own evidence what are commonly and
doubtless often correctly thought to be the authentic Shakespearean readings. This is as true for the preservation of
whole passages uniquely in Q2 or in F *Hamlet* as it is for the
question of the choice of *interr'd* or *enurn'd*.

Because of the corrupting (if not the revising) process in
manuscript transmission before the state of printer's copy is
reached, and because of the corrupting influence of the
transmission into print of this copy, the recovery and
authentication of Shakespeare's text must always proceed
from multiple authority by eclectic means. Let us not
mistake the bibliographical contribution to textual criticism.
Under no circumstances is it designed to substitute other
means for eclecticism. Instead, as I have tried to illustrate
throughout this chapter, textual bibliography takes as its
end the logical scientific control of the eclectic method and
the supplementing of the methods of literary criticism
applied to choice of readings. The control takes the form of
requiring the purely critical judgement to operate within
certain fixed bounds of physical fact and logical probability.

This union of the critical judgement with the bibliographical method is the hope for the future. Bibliography
alone will carry one a long way towards good editing, but it
is no magic carpet to the Promised Land. And if undue
expectation is aroused that it will solve all problems, the
disappointment will be the keener. It is true that less harm
than usual may be caused to a text if the bibliographical
method alone is narrowly followed; but for the real principles

of editing, for the discipline that places editing as almost a creative art, bibliography is only one of a triad that also includes language study but above all literary criticism shaping the judgement *within certain limits prescribed by bibliography and language.* It is a true remark of Sir Walter Greg's that often more misplaced ingenuity is devoted to defending a wrong reading than to emending it. In the history of Shakespearean editing—especially in the twentieth century when a *little* bibliography has sometimes become a rather dangerous thing—I should prefer the taste and judgement of a Kittredge (wrong as he sometimes was), and of an Alexander, to the unskilled and therefore unscientific operation of a scientific method as if it were the whole answer to the problem and automatically relieved an editor of the necessity to use his critical judgement in any way. Bibliography can only help to prepare a text for the final operation. Bibliography is a good servant but a bad master.

IV

PRINCIPLE AND PRACTICE IN THE EDITING OF EARLY DRAMATIC TEXTS

THE nineteenth-century editors of Elizabethan drama did not invent the modernised general-purpose reading edition: they were in the direct line of inheritance from the Shakespearean editors headed by Rowe, Pope, Theobald, and Malone. It would seem that the earliest editors never considered any other procedure. Indeed, the editorial 'purifying' (i.e. emending and modernising) of late sixteenth- and early seventeenth-century texts as represented by Shakespeare was only the natural carrying-forward, with some refinement, of Elizabethan commercial reprint practice, whereby each new edition became in effect a modernisation. Nor were printing-house editors unknown in the seventeenth century. The Shaaber–Black inquiry into the texts of the Second, Third, and Fourth Folios indicates quite clearly that the editing of Shakespeare did not begin with Rowe.

Various reasons may be assigned for this eighteenth- and nineteenth-century editorial ideal of the reading edition. The editing of the classics—which profoundly influenced the treatment of the vernacular—dictated modernisation and the flexible, eclectic treatment of texts. Also, the general distrust then prevalent of the conditions under which Elizabethan dramatic texts had found their way into print did not encourage respect for the precise forms in which these texts had been preserved in the extant documents. And, finally, the distinction had not yet developed between the general and the critical or scholarly reader. Although cultivated men were interested in the vernacular literature of the past, it had not yet become the prey of professional academic inquiry. Hence an effort to offer to the general interested reader editions in forms other than that to which he was accustomed would likely have been resisted as mere antiquarianism.

The growing scholarly interest of the nineteenth century in Elizabethan drama, and especially in Shakespeare, did not at first affect these general texts, since it was assumed that specialist critics would automatically require type-facsimiles like the Booth First Folio, or photographic facsimiles like the Halliwell-Phillipps or, later, the Lee First Folio, and the Praetorius Shakespeare quartos. The Old Cambridge edition of Shakespeare in the mid-1860's, with its collational lists of variants keyed to a modernised eclectic text, was for its time the summation of all that a literary critic could reasonably expect in textual scholarship. It is worth notice that the popular Globe reading text was substantially the same, without the collations on the text-pages.

Some interest in old-spelling texts had been shown in the late nineteenth century. Organisations like the Roxburghe Club, or private individuals like Grosart, printed versions of early texts—chiefly non-dramatic—in severely limited editions. Although the appeal was frequently to the anti-quarian, or to the book collector, some thought was apparently given to the dissemination of literary texts so rare as to be generally unavailable in their originals, or so scarce that an insurance against accident was in the nature of a public service. The scholars had their societies, of course, like the Early English Text Society or the Spenser Society. In more popular form, the Arber reprints of non-dramatic texts gave wide circulation in old spelling to a number of minor literary works of the past; and the curious Pearson reprints of the 1870's seemingly anticipated some popular interest in dramatic texts in old-spelling form.

Perhaps the earliest Elizabethan dramatic texts edited in a way that approached modern scholarly standards were such Oxford volumes as Boas's *Kyd* in 1901, or Bond's *Lyly* in 1902, or Tucker Brooke's *Marlowe* in 1910, all in old spelling; nor may we overlook the volumes of Bang's *Materialien zur Kunde des älteren Englischen Dramas* beginning in the first decade of this century. The editing now seems to be somewhat elementary in its method; nevertheless, these Oxford texts set a general style that has prevailed ever since for all serious editions of non-Shakespearean drama. The critical old-spelling edition that they led to may properly be called the peculiar invention of the twentieth century, and as such its rationale is worth some analysis.

A critical old-spelling edition attempts to establish the text of the literary work concerned and thereby to become a definitive edition.

Sir Walter Greg remarks that a critical edition is a 'critic's edition' in opposition to a popular or reading edition.[1] Clearly, he intends to distinguish an edition that will provide a complete, correct, and accurate textual basis for critical inquiry. We may be sure that to some degree no facsimile or reprint of any single most authoritative document (or parallel text of multiple substantive documents) fulfils these conditions. To require a literary critic to solve all the complex textual problems involved in the press-variant formes of Dekker's *Match Me in London*, for instance, before he can feel safe in quoting any part of the text in a study of the play's merits is as ridiculous as it would be to insist that a literary critic should accept *in toto* either the Folio or the Second Quarto text of *Hamlet*, and, if he revolted, to force him to decide from parallel texts the relationship and the authority of every variant reading before he dared to quote a speech in support of a character-analysis.

A text suitable for a critic must, inevitably, be an established text. Hence an edition is critical in the second sense that critical principles have been applied to the textual raw material of the authoritative preserved documents in order to approach as nearly as may be to the ideal of the authorial fair copy by whatever necessary process of recovery, independent emendation, or conflation of authorities. Such a critical edition is certainly a reading edition in that a critic need not interrupt his study of the significance of the edited text in order to solve for himself problems of its authenticity in substance or in form. However, it may also merit the name of 'critic's edition' in that its apparatus contains all the necessary evidence about the relation of the edited text to the authoritative documents used as raw-material in its preparation whenever the critic may wish to assure himself of the precise readings of the documents upon which the edited text is directly based.

So far as he can, the editor of a critical text attempts to recover as many characteristics as possible from the available evidence in order to reconstruct the lost printer's copy; and if this reconstructed copy proves to be deficient, he must attempt to recover characteristics of manuscripts antecedent to the copy (as in the case of *The Merry Wives of Windsor*). The resulting text—of necessity—cannot reproduce in all its details any extant document, since the method by which it was contrived must be eclectic.[1]

The fearsomeness attached to this word *eclectic* is difficult to understand. On the one hand, as Greg has pointed out, the distrust of eclecticism—though representative of a conservative reaction to past excesses—can be carried too far.[2] The fundamental mistake of the eighteenth- and nineteenth-century editors of the Elizabethan drama, was, in his words, 'not so much that they were prepared on occasion to introduce into the copy-text [or what they on the whole treated as such] readings from other sources, as that in doing so they relied upon personal predilection instead of critical analysis'.

It would seem high time that the bugaboos of eighteenth- and nineteenth-century eclectic excesses were allowed to deflate peaceably and that literate users should become convinced that present standards of eclectic editing are founded on very different principles from those of a Gifford. Greg's discussion of modern eclecticism is eminently sane and balanced,[3] but now needs to be supplemented by reference to more strictly bibliographical principles for determining the authority of individual readings, a technique that had not been developed very fully at the date of his remarks. For example, when in 1933 Hazelton Spencer came to Dekker's *Honest Whore*, Part I, in his *Elizabethan Plays*, an anthology that for its day was most conscientiously edited (far in advance of conventional practice for anthologies twenty years later), his use of the then newly discovered second edition was still eclectic in the old-fashioned sense, since he had not solved the bibliographical problem of the exact printing relationship between the two editions, the retention of standing type from the first in the second edition, and the differing relationship of the variants in the standing type from those in the reset type. Thus he could not define the respective authority of each edition, page by page, and so could not explain why in some places the second edition seemed inferior but in others manifestly superior. Failing here, he had no possible criterion other than personal taste to guide him in the choice of readings from among the numerous variants, and it was inevitable that he should not be correct in all cases.

In comparison, present-day bibliographical techniques distinguish the use in this second edition of corrected standing type from the first, and of reset type; and then proceed to analyse the textual characteristics of the variants in each according to the bibliographical units of the different sheets printed in three different shops. The bibliographical explanation of the evidence suggests why in the work of only one shop the reset formes contain authoritative revisions and corrections, although the standing formes in all shops were authoritatively corrected. Thus the problem of the authority of the several classes of variants is solved according to the mechanical evidence of the printing process. Consequently, editorial eclecticism in the choice of variants now from one and now from the other edition becomes quite automatic, completely demonstrable, and not subject in the least to differences of critical opinion.[1]

The development of compositorial analysis from its recent pioneering successes may be expected to open many new approaches to the bibliographical determination of authority in individual readings. When from our knowledge of the

specific habits of the compositors who governed the transmission we can rear a solid foundation of fact to support
conjecture about the authenticity of readings, we shall have
gone a long way towards the recovery of the characteristics
of the lost original, beyond the dreams of even ten years ago.

The error made by extreme conservatives in textual
matters is to suppose that any kind of editorial intervention
will distort a text and erect some barrier between the critic
and the original purity of the most authoritative preserved
form of an author's words. Instead, we should take the
guiding principle of the critically edited text to be the
restoration of the closest communication between author
and reader by removing the barriers of error in the preserved documents. These originals will certainly be corrupt
in some details simply because they hold transmitted forms
of the text.

In theory this end is so reasonable, and even desirable,
that the question arises why all texts are not like this. What
is it that prevents a critical reading edition from being used
as a general, or popular reading edition?

Various answers may be given, of various degrees of pertinence. For example, it is not enough to remark that critical
editions are ordinarily constructed according to higher
standards of scholarship than popular reading editions. The
statement is true, but it is true only in practice: no principle
necessitates an inferior standard for the popular edition.
There is nothing in the nature of the general reading public
so depraved as to prompt it to demand bad texts. No
principle save lack of principle and its concomitant carelessness requires the editors of our numerous anthologies of
Elizabethan plays to seek their printer's copy from corrupt

nineteenth-century editions (or modern copies of these) rather than from a fresh survey of the original documents.

One may also remark that it used to be the fashion to load a critical edition with such an imposing mass of apparatus on each page that a general reader might well have flinched at the prospect of finding his way through this underbrush, let alone having to pay for its printing. But such a parade of textual learning—most of it worthless, incidentally, even to the professional literary critic—is now out of fashion, and means have been found to associate with the text-page only the data of immediate importance, the rest (of specialised interest) being placed in decent obscurity where it may be consulted by those whom the editors of the past used to distinguish as 'the curious'. It is amusing to notice that a popular reading edition of Shakespeare, the New Arden, which retains from its original design the old-fashioned display of textual variants on an historical principle, offers to its general reader much more of such apparatus on the text-page than the Cambridge critical edition of Thomas Dekker, which by its subject is addressed primarily to a more learned audience.

Seemingly the real point of distinction is whether an early text is modernised for popular readers or allowed to remain in its old-spelling dress for critics and other learned folk.

As a theory, the preservation in any serious edition of the old-spelling characteristics of a text, whether of the sixteenth or of the eighteenth century, scarcely needs defence. Arguments in its favour may stress the positive virtues of retention, or—negatively—the difficulties and inconsistencies resulting from modernisation. Among the foremost of the positive arguments, to my way of thinking, is this. An historical or critical scholar requires a text in which there has been no unnecessary interposition between him and the words of an author in their most authoritative form. The phrase 'most authoritative form' must be taken as applying in two senses: first, the words themselves and their arrangements; and, secondly, the system of spelling, punctuation, and capitalisation in which the words in their arrangements present themselves.

Once we temper the too violent reaction to the faulty conventions on which early editors based their eclecticism, and do not confuse bad practice with good principle, we may view the cult of the single, most authoritative original document with clearer eyes. And viewing this equally faulty counter-reaction at its true value, we may grant that the problem of the 'most authoritative words' cannot be solved by facsimile or facsimile-style reprint texts which in their conservatism provide no more than textual raw material to the critic. The eclectic effort to recover from the transmitted documents the exact wording of the author's lost original does not constitute unnecessary editorial interposition, we may continue to grant, so long as its principles are critically, linguistically, and bibliographically sound. The question then arises: what constitutes unnecessary editorial intervention in the second element of a text—the spelling, punctuation, capitalisation, and word division, what Greg calls the 'accidents' of a text?

The answer would appear to be the logical one: any interference with (1) the author's intentions in these matters, (2) the specific transmitting agent's intentions when these do not appear to clash with what may be supposed to have been the author's intentions, and (3) the general orthographic

habits of the period contemporary with the most authoritative transmitted forms of the accidentals of the copy-text,
when these do not appear to clash with (1) or with (2) above.

It is clear that only a fairly conservative reproduction
of the old-spelling characteristics of an Elizabethan dramatic
text will satisfy these three requirements. Very briefly, the
arguments may be elaborated.

(1) The example of Ben Jonson, with his scrupulous
regard for the presentation in print of his accidentals, is
scarcely typical of the attitude of the usual Elizabethan
dramatist. Presumably most authors—including the few
who had any control over the printing of their plays—were
content to accept the form the printing-house imposed on
their accidentals, so long as the meaning was not vitally
affected. In this they differed no whit from most authors in
any age. The authenticated presence of a proof-reading
author is most uncommon in the publishing history of
Elizabethan dramatic quartos. Yet the few cases that have
come to my attention in which I felt there was some reason
to attribute press-variants to an author in the Dekker plays
have indicated that when an Elizabethan dramatist did overlook the work of a compositor, he was by no means indifferent to the system of capitalisation, punctuation,
spelling, and word-division that had been imposed on his
copy. Hence it would seem that real grounds exist for
a critic's concern to read a text in a form as close as may be
to the author's system of accidentals as well as substantives.
Certainly, in view of the changes made in capitalisation in
the first stage of correction of forme inner A and outer L in
Match Me in London, variants that I attribute to Dekker,
it is not mere fantasy to argue that something of an author's

individuality may be conveyed in the accidentals of his printed works. The question is, however, are a sufficient number of these transmitted in a dramatic quarto to make an attempt at their preservation worthwhile?

(2) In considerable part we do not know whether an appreciable number of a dramatic author's accidentals are really transmitted by a compositor. Moreover, it is unsafe to generalise, since preliminary investigation has disclosed that some compositors are much more faithful to these characteristics of their copy than others. Finally, we are much handicapped by having no Elizabethan example of manuscript printer's copy for a play so that a test case can be analysed. We are able to assess compositors from their treatment of reprints, but we cannot be at all certain that a given compositor's practice when setting from printed copy would coincide with his habits when setting from manuscript. Indeed, we may suppose that an almost automatic difference could exist in that the 'styling' necessary to put some printing-house form on a manuscript is not required of the compositor of a reprint.

However, some tentative conclusions may be drawn from the very few investigations that have been made.

(*a*) When no great interval has elapsed between the original print and its reprint, the statistical evidence suggests that some compositors were inclined to follow the accidentals of their *printed* copy with more conservatism than individuality.

(*b*) Spelling tests applied to identified compositors are likely to show that there are comparatively few words or linguistic forms in which an invariable spelling is so significant as to suggest habitual compositorial practice. For instance, although the differentiation of compositors *A* and *B* in the Shakespeare First Folio is not confined to the familiar *do*, *go*, *here* variants, the ascertained habitual variations between them are not large. I do not suggest by any means that the majority of the indifferent forms represents the printer's copy; but I take it that there is some cause to hope that in many dramatic quartos there is a proportion large enough to be called significant in which *known* compositorial habit does not overlay the texture of the original.[1]

(*c*) That in some cases the accidentals of the copy may on the whole exercise more influence on compositors than is often believed may be suggested by the observation that when two identified compositors in one play set another text, their differentiating characteristics may somewhat shift, perhaps indicating the influence of copy.[2]

(*d*) In cases when close examination has been made, encouraging results have followed a study of the manner in which specific accidentals have filtered through the typesetting of one or more compositors (if by 'encouraging' is understood that *some* penetration of the copy may be observed even though it is far from a general show-through). As a rule, the proportion of hyphenated compounds in Dekker texts may be so high as to lead one to suspect this hyphenation to be a characteristic of his manuscripts. I take it as significant, therefore, that in the collaborated *Virgin Martyr* (1622) the single compositor sets as many as fifteen such hyphens in some Dekker scenes and scarcely a hyphen in Massinger's known scenes. Because it concerns a minor characteristic, such evidence is more telling as an indication of compositorial faithfulness to copy than, in the same play, the use of the digraph *æ* in the spelling of the name

Cæsarea in the Massinger scenes, but the letter *e* (*Cesarea*) in the Dekker. Yet this same compositor, though so faithful in these and a few other respects, does very little about transmitting such Massinger characteristics as may be observed in the holograph manuscript for his *Believe As You List* (though this is of considerably later date) despite the evidence which suggests that a Massinger autograph probably directly underlies his scenes in *The Virgin Martyr* print. And except for a very few matters, no orthographical differences can be seen in the Massinger as against the Dekker scenes in the *Martyr* quarto.

It is obvious that in some major part the intentions of the compositor—as manifested in the forms of the accidentals in his typesetting—are not always at one with the author, since the compositor may impose some few of his own orthographic habits on these accidentals in so distinctive a way as to enable us to use his few habitual spellings as evidence for identifying him. On the other hand, like the compositor of *The Virgin Martyr*, he may overlay the divergent orthography of two authors with his own often indifferent system of spelling in a way that almost completely obscures their respective individuality. Some compositors, but not others, may attempt to reproduce a few of the accidental forms of the manuscript, as noticed by Dr Philip Williams and Dr Hoy in the examples given in the previous chapter. Some compositors' practice may be relatively indifferent,[1] and hence copy may be followed, in part, more by fortune than design; but, nevertheless, whether fortuitously or not, in some part an author's accidentals may be transmitted in sufficient measure, *small as it may usually be*, for us to feel that they are a matter of legitimate concern.

The example of *The Virgin Martyr* does not promote optimism about the number that will be transmitted (and certainly no valid linguistic study could be made of its two authors from this print); yet the few that can be distinguished are sufficient to determine the authorship of the various scenes and even, in one case, to lead to the hypothesis that Dekker partly revised a scene originally by Massinger. Similar assessments have been made in other plays, by Dr Hoy and Dr Waller. Hence the conclusion that must be emphasised (since it could easily be mistaken) is this: the individual characteristics of an author's accidentals that filter through into a print may statistically be very few, but they can be of extraordinary service to a critic, out of all proportion to their number. This significance cannot be used, however, as evidence for such a general distribution of authorial characteristics in a print as to justify linguists like Wyld and Kökeritz in assuming the detailed similarity of print to underlying manuscript.

(3) Even if we had no positive evidence that the accidentals of an author have been transmitted in any significant manner, there is still reason for a critic to prefer the form given to a text by a contemporary printing-house instead of the form of a modernisation. Greg very pertinently argues: 'For the critic modernization has no attraction in itself. So long as there is any chance of an edition preserving some trace, however faint, of the author's individuality, the critic will wish to follow it: and even when there is none, he will still prefer an orthography that has a period resemblance with the author's to one that reflects the linguistic habits of a later date'.[1]

It is certainly an open question whether the process of

modernisation does not 'unnecessarily' produce editorial interference between a critic and the original. Greg remarks, 'That modernization on the lines usually followed does quite seriously misrepresent Elizabethan English, experience has amply proved'.[1] If a critic of an Elizabethan text wants to read it in Elizabethan English, as he should, he cannot take his chances with modernising editors. A moderniser has only two choices—to be partial or complete—and both distort the text that a critic will use. The editor of a partially modernised text like the New Arden may retain the original spellings of such forms of words as appear to him to be distinct; but he will be no more consistent than the New Yale editors who have been instructed to retain such original forms as, in their opinion, represent a difference in pronunciation—a hopeless task. In either case, experience shows the impossibility of controlling any method of partial modernisation without serious inconsistency. What one editor feels to be distinct forms may not appear to be so to another:[2] one editor may present to the critic as linguistically significant a mixture of essentially meaningful and meaningless forms;[3] the other may conceal meaningful forms through his ignorance or misconception.[4] The editor who attempts to use assumed pronunciation as a guide is no better off. (A bibliographer must ask, *whose* pronunciation and *whose* orthography theoretically reflecting pronunciation? Do such editors suppose that inconsistency within the same text invariably reflects distinctive pronunciations intended for the speaker of the lines or the reader of the print?)

The linguistic problems involved in partial modernisation are bad enough, but to them we must add the bibliographical problems. Is the random use of *murder* and *murther* in a text, for example, the product of the writer's phonological in-difference; that is, did no distinction in pronunciation occur to the author? Is it the result of compositorial indifference watering down a systematic and unified authorial form? Or is it an outright clash between two different systematic conventions in which the author's form occasionally filters through the overlay of the compositor's? The answer can well differ for any individual text, and under most circum-stances would be far beyond the editor's grasp. Hence any system of partial modernisation is based on a false con-fidence about the scope of our present knowledge and is bound seriously to mislead a critic either by superfluity of meaningless variation or by errors of concealment. A fake Elizabethan English results, fake because many of the forms selected for preservation are not in truth more than ortho-graphically variant. That is, every partially modernising editor deceives the critic in some respects about the author's language by offering as meaningful variants what are often no more than indifferent alternative spellings which, at least in the text in question, have lost any pronunciation dif-ferences they may have had, or—otherwise—have no signifi-cance as any longer representing distinct forms of linguistic concern.[1]

Conscious of these difficulties, a new school asserts that—whatever the problems—the only consistency lies in com-plete and absolute modernisation.[2] My own sympathies lie here, since cutting has its obvious attractions when such a knot is presented. On the other hand, although an editor may thereby avoid offering to the critic a mishmash of significant and non-significant forms, emphasised by their retention in an otherwise modernised text, he cannot escape the accusation that he has concealed even more significant evidence about Elizabethan speech than the partial-modernising editor.

In this matter of what is significant evidence—what is the Elizabethan English that a critic really needs and that is destroyed by complete modernisation—opinions may well differ.[1] Clearly, we can trust a present-day editor (we hope) not to convert *'em* to *them* as Gifford did, or silently to restore concord of subject and verb as was customary with Dyce and earlier editors, and to avoid any other tinkering with real linguistic forms if in fact such alteration is in all cases possible to avoid.[2] I do not myself feel that a completely modernising editor need regret his smoothing-out of possible variant Elizabethan pronunciations (rhyme words constitute a separate problem). In some cases the variant orthography may indicate actual variant pronunciation; in others, the variant orthography undoubtedly has nothing to do with actual speech. Hence, since there is some general agreement that our linguistic information is still too deficient for us to be positive about the relation of the orthography to the phonology in most dramatic texts, the completely modernising editor has two advantages over his partially modernising colleague, namely:

(1) Full modernisation escapes the anomaly of requiring readers to pronounce certain words in an approximately Elizabethan manner when the orthography suggests variance, but allowing them to pronounce in the modern manner others which, orthography or no, would have been differently pronounced by an Elizabethan. A sceptic might well inquire what is gained by this arbitrary distinction when, admittedly, we cannot trust the orthography to reflect differences with

accuracy; and at best we can force a reader to shape his pronunciation to the text for only a selection of words.

(2) Full modernisation escapes the anomaly of forcing a modern reader to pronounce some words in two ways, according to the vagaries of the early text, and thus of distinguishing as meaningful what was ordinarily unintentional and inoperative. That is, when in adjacent lines one can find the spelling *murther* and also *murder* in a speech by the same dramatic character, surely it is ridiculous to require a modern reader to distinguish in pronunciation the variant orthographic forms that would certainly *not* have been distinguished by the Elizabethan actor, or by the author reading his own lines. Under Elizabethan repertory conditions no actor could possibly memorise and reproduce such minutiae, even if anyone could discern what purpose would be served. And whether an author would casually pronounce the variants as they were spelled has yet to be proved.

It is proper to survey what may be lost by full modernisation. Some of the loss is more apparent than real. So long as we recognise what audience we are addressing in a modernised text and do not make the mistake of assuming that it is a learned one, we can drop without regret all dialectal (or misprint) variants like *band–bond* which have the same immediate etymology, or like *tatter–totter* which have a more remote common etymology, when the use is complementary and no distinction in meaning is effected by the appearance of one or the other form.[1] In a modernised text it is doubtless mere sentimentality to attempt to retain assumed authorial usage in one or other variant form of the same word like *band–bond*; and, of course, many of these variants do not actually reflect the author's own intentions or usage.

I would not myself feel any sense of loss in failing to distinguish Marcellus' *Illo* from Hamlet's *Hillo* one line apart. I very much doubt that Shakespeare intended one pronunciation to be characteristic of Marcellus and the other of Hamlet; and to imply to a modern reader that he did—as editors do by retaining the different spellings in a modernised text—seems to me to be simple folly, the more especially since *Illo* is very likely a contaminated form from the bad First Quarto, passed on to Q2 and repeated from it in the Folio.

The greatest loss to actual Elizabethan English occurs when full modernisation—to be consistent—must obliterate not a mere dialectal form but a really distinctive obsolete word, such as I take *sally* (for *sully*) to be; but etymological grounds cannot be consistently employed to justify partial modernisation.

A fully modernised text, therefore, accepts the fact that its users will be reading the words throughout with a modern pronunciation. It is content, therefore, to relinquish any attempt to transfer Elizabethan phonology to the present day when meaning—which is to say, intent—is not affected. When by confusion, analogy, or whatever cause, distinct words have fused, or are in the process of fusing, and their two forms no longer convey a different meaning or shade of meaning in the text itself, the only intentional use of one or other form will ordinarily be in puns or in humorous dialectal speech. Otherwise, phonological differences must be erased in modernised texts. Morphological differences are, of course, conventionally retained although I should not myself like to defend all cases on logical grounds. It seems pretty clear that in some texts the distinction, say, between the verb endings -*s*, -*st*, and -*eth* is merely orthographical and no actual difference in pronunciation would obtain. According to present practice, however, the loss to the reader from modernisation is almost exclusively phonological. But so many small details in any original must be altered that it can scarcely be said that in many respects the idiom, usage, and flavour of an older speech are actually retained in any modernised text, no matter how careful the editing.[1]

In this connection the punctuation and its problems cannot be neglected. Joseph Moxon's advice to his late seventeenth-century compositors to consider the sense of the copy carefully as an aid to pointing it is a sufficient indication that punctuation was, in general, the province of the printing-house; and it is no accident that the majority of the alterations ordered in press by the printing-house proof-readers refer to the punctuation. The erratic (or almost non-existent) punctuation often found in the dramatic manuscripts of the period no doubt justifies Greg's conclusion: 'It might at times strike us as effective, but it would probably be unreliable. And as a rule the compositor probably paid little attention to it. It may be that some striking instances of dramatic pointing that critics have discovered in early editions do in fact represent sudden inspirations of the author, though it is likely that they have survived more or less by chance in a general system (such as it is) imposed upon the text in the printing-house.'[2]

Under these conditions when even an old-spelling editor is urged to exercise more freedom with an ordinarily unreliable medium of communication (i.e. unreliable in its authority), a modernising editor might be expected to treat the early pointing with even less reverence. Generally, almost absolute freedom has obtained, but in some respects editorial treatment of the punctuation has been the least satisfactory of the different processes of modernisation. The reason is not far to seek. Whereas spelling modernised according to the system of Dr Johnson's day, for example, still uses substantially the same conventions as ours, or so close as to cause no difficulty, fashions of punctuation have altered radically with the passage of time. What was the satisfactory modernised system of pointing for Dr Johnson, with its heavy syntactical notation and its free use of exclamation marks, is not a satisfactory guide for the present-day reader, even though he is still in large part forced to submit to it in Shakespearean texts.

In revolt against the heavy hand of eighteenth-century standards of punctuation, distrustful of the comparatively rapid obsolescence of any modernised punctuation system, and infected with the optimistic view that the pointing of an early print may substantially reflect the author's own intentions, in some detail, an occasional editor has modernised the Elizabethan text in respect to spelling, capitalisation, and such matters, but has retained in very considerable part the original punctuation,[1] as for example the New Arden *Antony and Cleopatra*. It is not simple antiquarianism, I hope, to protest that this is a most unsatisfactory practice, that the accidentals of a text are of a piece and should be uniformly treated, and that an obsolete system of pointing clashes psychologically (even practically) with modern spelling.

More pertinent, for an important part of the communication of meaning reliance has been placed on a system

unfamiliar to the general reader. In addition, this pointing—
the one part of the original accidentals thus singled out for
reproduction—is on the whole the most unreliable of all the
transmitted characteristics. That is, here if anywhere the
characteristics of the print seem likely to reflect the intentions of the early compositor(s) and proof-reader(s) instead
of the author, and the preservation of these characteristics
in the midst of modernisation puts a most disproportionate
value upon them. In most cases we may suppose that there
was no positive clash between the printing-house punctuation and the author's general intentions except for examples
of complete misunderstanding; but we must not suppose
that the printing-house has faithfully mirrored these intentions, especially in such refined matters as critics are
likely to accept for particular comment. Any blinding
illumination of the subtleties of meaning in a dramatic text,
therefore, is not likely to come from a sudden insight into
the peculiar appropriateness of a punctuation mark, or its
absence.[1]

Finally, one may protest that the Elizabethan system of
punctuation is not the modern one. To a person accustomed
to the meaning transmitted by the shorthand of modern
syntactical pointing, the Elizabethan rhetorical system with
its quite different values attached to the marks in the
weighting of pause through commas, semi-colons, and colons
is at least as confusing as would be the presentation of the
words in their original spelling. Any reader sophisticated
enough to read Elizabethan punctuation without a sense of
strangeness, or of insecurity, is capable of handling a text
in old spelling. And a reader familiar with Elizabethan
punctuation can never be conscious of other than a futile

anachronism when this pointing is retained in modern spelling.[1]

In their antiquarian attachment to obsolete punctuation, as if it somehow conveyed more of the rhetorical intentions of the author, modern editors show that they are unaware of the capacities of their audience. Since present-day punctuation is much lighter and more suggestive than that of a generation or so ago, a modernising editor would be well advised to translate into the syntactical and pause system familiar to all his readers—according to the most forward-looking contemporary standards of indicating rapidity or slowness—whatever may be his private conception of the intentions of his copy-text in its own differently styled rhetorical or quasi-syntactical system.

Complete modernisation must govern the punctuation as well as the other parts of the accidentals: it is absurd to argue that Elizabethan flexibility and rapidity cannot be indicated by especially light modern pointing. And if an editor protests that owing to the changes of fashion in punctuation his version will in due course become out-dated in this respect, one can only answer that such has been the fate of all modernisations, from the Shakespeare Second Folio of 1632 onwards. It is only proper for each generation to have a modernised text that in its accidentals corresponds to what is usual and ordinary at the time. It is very much an anachronism that so many of our present-day modernised texts retain the heavy eighteenth-century style of pointing because of the indolence of editors unwilling to take the trouble to alter the pointing of the out-of-date edition they have chosen to send to the printer.

This survey of the problems that attend the presentation

to modern readers of the texts of Elizabethan dramatists has endeavoured to suggest that:

(1) Valuable as is the photographic or the type facsimile (or the diplomatic reprint), it remains a specialist's tool; and since it can do no more than reflect the text in its raw and inevitably imperfect state, it is not suitable for general critical use as the alternative to the modernised text.

(2) The partially or completely modernised text may be a present-day commercial necessity for school-children and even (though this I deny) for the undergraduate. But at best it cannot serve as a critical basis for a serious student for whom the specific characteristics of a text should have an interest.

It would appear, therefore, that there is a need for a class of text aimed at an audience somewhere between the bibliographical or textual specialist and the school-child. This need may be filled by properly constructed critical old-spelling editions. At the upper level these editions should be qualified to serve as trustworthy foundations for advanced critical inquiry; at the lower level it should not be beyond the ability of a literate undergraduate to handle them.

Clear thinking in this matter is of real importance, because the drift to popularisation is causing a certain amount of confusion. Let us put to one side what is sometimes called 'the Shakespeare industry' with its flood of competing cheap texts aimed indiscriminately at the schools, the required undergraduate studies, and that many-headed being, the 'general reader'. There will always be a need for popular modernised Shakespeare texts. Let us grant it, and hope that they will improve. But let us not forget that it has been the pressure of these modernised texts that, to the point of open scandal, has left us without any complete old-spelling Shakespeare edited according to critical principles and suitable for critical purposes.

May we not lay this down as a doctrine? In all cases when a definitive edition is proposed for a dramatist, or other author, of no matter what century, we should insist (*a*) that it be critically edited, and (*b*) that in its texture of accidentals, as well as in its words, it conform to the closest approximation to the author's own linguistic and orthographic characteristics that can be recovered.

If such an edition is available, it will have a double function. It will serve as a reading text for the critically inclined, and it will establish the text for whatever modernised versions may prove to be commercially necessary. The latter function scarcely needs comment. We should not have collected editions of Shakespeare still substantially reprinting the Globe text, because the editors (for textbook and general reading purposes) feel incapable of grappling with the problems of the originals, if a good critically edited old-spelling edition were available to serve as a standard, and as a quarry. As for the first function, a critical reading edition must offer an established text. An established text is one that presents the works of an author in their most authoritative form in respect to (1) the words themselves and their arrangements; and (2) the system of spelling, punctuation, capitalisation, division, and the like, in which these words are found in the early document that has the closest transcriptional link with the lost holograph.[1] For editorial purposes, as Greg has demonstrated in a classic study,[2] the documents from which (1) and (2) are drawn may differ in the case of a revised edition authoritative on the whole for the altered verbals but less authoritative for the accidentals because further removed than the original print from holograph. Any text contrived on these principles should be a reading text and not meant merely for reference. Yet concessions to ease of reading should not be such as to destroy the general usefulness of an edition as an adequate substitute for the original documents (short of a searching bibliographical inquiry into the nature of the text and its transmission).

Let us be sensible about this matter. In various respects any such critically edited text cannot be a substitute for a photographic facsimile of the original document, or for the document itself.[1] But these respects are so few and so specialised that their requirements cannot properly affect the question of the general usefulness of the critical old-spelling edition. Let us grant that if a bibliographer wants to analyse the presswork of a book by studying the running-titles, or to determine the work of individual compositors by recording the passage of identified types in and out of the printer's cases, or to analyse the patterns of shortages of italic types in order to determine whether the pages were set *seriatim* or by formes, he must go to the originals or to photographs. Let us grant that many other close technical studies of a bibliographical nature cannot be managed from an edited text; and let us emphasise, also, that for these even a type facsimile like the Malone Society Reprints would be of only slightly greater use. Since no analytical bibliographer would dream of using an edited text for much of his basic work, it is not at all improper to ignore his special requirements except where they begin to impinge on those textual studies for which an old-spelling edition is satisfactory enough, at least provisionally. On the other hand, if an interested philologist wants to study certain language forms in early texts, it would be quite improper to require him to travel to distant libraries or to bear the expense of photographs and film, or of published reproductions when they exist, merely because the editor of a purportedly definitive edition has chosen to modernise. ('It is...only reasonable to allow weight to the demands of the philologist, who needs exact and reliable texts as a basis for the study of linguistic phenomena.'[1])

It would seem that the uses of an old-spelling text are so various and so widespread that the important information about the original documents that such an edition offers—not for reference only, but for reading as well—should not be lost through pressure for thoughtless popularisation based on the assumed demands of a general reading public. If we concentrate upon producing an edition that meets the requirements of the critic within as attractive a framework as we can contrive without damage to the essential critical information purveyed, we shall have achieved the most desirable product of modern textual scholarship. Moreover, the definition of the critic must not be unduly limited. A reader of a dramatic text in search of information about Elizabethan idiom, usage, possible and impossible spelling forms, morphological variants, techniques of plot construction, methods of characterisation, metrics, the author's use of hypermetrical lines, short lines, caesural pause, feminine endings, rhyme, syncopation of syllables, about contemporary printers' treatment of act and scene numbering, or authorial or compositorial treatment of stage-directions and their exact form, about dramatic morals, contemporary manners, stage conventions of entrance and exit, the circumstances of soliloquy, and so on and so on, such a reader is as much a critical user of the edition as the one who is concerned with the philosophical import of the theme of reconciliation in Shakespeare's last plays. If the ultimate consumers of a definitive text can range from philologists to students of stagecraft, it does not seem unreasonable to ask the general literary student to accept a few textual conventions for which the immediate application to his own problems may seem obscure.

But certainly we must not be too solemn about the so-called definitive edition, or the permanent establishment of any text,[1] and we must recognise with humility that many features of an old-spelling text are retained because of our ignorance, not because of our knowledge.[2] Perhaps in the future our bibliographical and philological equipment may enable another generation to overturn accepted standards of old-spelling editing; but the day is not yet, and a good old-spelling text is likely to age less than a good modernisation. Certainly, until this day of apocalyptic knowledge arrives we are as justified in refusing to normalise by modernisation as in refusing to normalise by making up a synthetic system of Elizabethan accidentals to which all texts must conform.

This ignorance, and the conservatism that, unfortunately, it promotes, is real; but we should not hinge the whole critical case for old spelling on it. The violence done to Elizabethan English, the impossibility either of consistency or of non-violence, in the process of altering the details of the accidentals without affecting to some degree the substantives that are a part of this texture, are arguments as weighty as those that come from the doctrine of despair. Therefore the literary critic (taking the term in its broadest sense) ought to have the maximum information provided him in a trustworthy form, and with the minimum of unnecessary editorial interference. And what is good enough for the critic ought to be good enough for the general reader.

However, let us continue to try to be sensible. It is to the advantage of any definitive edition which establishes a text to appeal to the largest possible group of users, so long as this catholicity is not achieved at the expense of critically dangerous modifications. A wider appeal for such an edition may be achieved (1) in questions relating to the details of the text itself, with particular reference to its old-spelling form; and (2) in questions relating to the presentation of the text, with particular reference to its apparatus and commentary.

(1) A critical old-spelling editor is accustomed to altering his copy-text so long as he provides a record of his departures from the original. It is not perhaps sufficiently recognised that he has, in fact, made a selection of the departures to record even when he thinks he has recorded *all* such departures. For example, any sensible editor of a text other than a type facsimile or diplomatic reprint—that is, any editor of a text addressed to a critic—will scarcely wish to burden his reader with details of wrong-fount letters and punctuation, of variable spacing, and other purely mechanical features of the typesetting which seem to him to have no critical significance. I believe he is right in this, for the only alternative is the photographic facsimile. Although wrong-fount letters may furnish the bibliographer with evidence of the most far-reaching significance in his estimate of the details of the printing process by which the text was

transmitted—evidence that may in the end apply with striking immediacy to the reliability of the text as a whole, or in relation to some specific reading (as with press-variants)— nevertheless, we should firmly hold that such investigation is part of the initial preparation of the established form of the text and is no part of general critical concern except in its completed, analysed, and applied form.

That is, we may take it that a critic should always be much concerned with the editor's estimate of the reliability of the original text, both as a whole and in any specified particular, and may even feel it necessary to understand the nature of the evidence upon which the bibliographical editor has based his assumptions, in order to estimate the full import of these editorial assumptions and their effect on the presentation of the text. But we may hold it to be no function of the editor to provide evidence for further basic bibliographical investigation which should, after all, have been completed as an essential part of the editing of the text. In other words, an editor must not expect his own weaknesses of analysis to be excused on the plea that he has printed evidence which enables the critic to do the job himself if he wishes. It is an anomaly for an editor proposing to establish a text to expect wiser heads to carry forward and then to apply the basic bibliographical examination of the document on which the very details of the establishment should have rested.[1] 'Every reader his own bibliographer' is an absurdity.

If then in some details a critical editor must perforce alter his original, silently, it behoves us to inquire what else he may alter that is of little or no import save in the basic preparation of the text, and completed before publication. Much he must emend and record, of course, as the very essential of the recovery of the author's intentions—on the available evidence—from their transmitted form, or of the transmitting agent's intentions, or of the practice of the time. This is the process that distinguishes the critically edited text from the mere reprint or the facsimile. But if the resulting text is to attract the largest number of readers, it is likely that some regularising of purely typographical details[1] will remove a certain part of the old-spelling strangeness and assist in the acceptance of the text as a reading edition by more readers. Such acceptance is a desirable end: it is not necessarily the height of scholarship to produce an edition of value chiefly for reference.

This is not the place to specify all the precise details that may be regularised, whether silently or with notation.[2] In general, it may be said that typographical details that could not have appeared in the underlying manuscript are normalised with little loss if they would otherwise prove intrusive or distracting. It is mere pedantry, surely, to attempt to reproduce (as if it had any significance) the fact that in the original a particular scene begins with a two-line or a three-line display capital, or that such and such a letter combination was ligatured, or that a *w* was formed as *vv*. The editor may surely be allowed to treat in a typographically uniform way the founts in which the names of characters are set, whether in speech-prefixes, stage-directions, or the text. And so on. The more violent anomalies of Elizabethan punctuation may surely be his concern as much as they were the concern of the contemporary proof-reader. And he will surely wish to divide the lines of verse in what appears to be the correct way, indenting when a speech begins with the completion of a line as Capell was the first to do.

10-2

McKerrow, though reluctantly, modernised the Elizabethan long f; and this procedure has now become standard
in old-spelling critical texts. Surely an editor should
seriously consider normalising the u:v and i:j complements
in early texts.[1] There can be no doubt that to the general
reader these letters are as marked a stumbling block as was
the old long f; and we should do well to ask ourselves why
we retain them if in doing so we keep up a real bar to the
more general use of old-spelling texts, and indeed almost
deliberately encourage modernised editions. Since there is
every practical reason for this reform in old-spelling texts
and—if I understand the matter correctly—no real linguistic anomaly, the normalisation of these letters may be
urged for critical texts, whatever the value of their retention
in facsimile or diplomatic texts.

(2) The second way in which old-spelling texts may be
made more popular with a general audience concerns the
apparatus. If we grant that a critical edition should be
primarily a reading edition and only secondarily a reference
edition, then we should simplify the ease and attractiveness
of reading by reducing the apparatus appearing on the
type-page and placing the larger part of it elsewhere for
reference. The text-page of a critical edition is not the proper
place for collations of rejected readings from unauthoritative or rejected sources (that is, for an historical list of
variants). It is pertinent to inform the reader directly by
a note at the foot of the page when an editor has altered
some substantive readings in his copy-text. Yet if the
normalisation of accidentals of a kind that should be recorded may be removed in some texts to an appendix, how
much less justification is there for continually distracting

the user from his business of reading the established text by inviting him to contemplate lists of variant words (and sometimes mere punctuations) that the editor has rejected from a series of sources that have only historical interest. We may presume that the editor is not so uncertain about his rejection as to feel it obligatory to offer the reader the constant opportunity to check him by selecting what readings he chooses from unauthoritative editions as legitimate alternatives to the readings of the edited and established text. (Every reader his own textual critic?) If not, these lists of variants are useless except for reference and have no place on the text-page of a reading, not a reference edition. Such a parade of learning was well enough in the days when only scholars (who will put up with anything) were supposed to read old-spelling editions; but now it is anachronistic and absurd. To read a text properly not even a scholarly user needs to have under his eye the whole record of corruption of the authoritative words through a series of reprints and previously edited versions of the text.

The problem of the old-spelling critical edition, therefore, is to maintain itself by a series of logical compromises as both a learned and a general reading text. These compromises affect its form and its presentation. What we should understand is that these compromises affect only the form and presentation and do not lower the quality of the edition or its principles. A critical edition is not the bastard child of a facsimile or reprint text; if it is properly contrived it is an improvement, in that it more faithfully represents the author's intentions than any reproduction of a single transmitted documentary form can do. Once scholars recognise this principle and reject the reprint fetish for the texts of printed books as vigorously as Housman rejected it for manuscripts, the intellectual way can be prepared for a clearer discussion of the means of presenting these critical texts in the most suitable form to a larger public

It is a shameful thing that we are bringing up a generation of undergraduates and other readers who are scarcely conscious that the language of the past differed in its forms from that of the present, that Shakespeare did not write in logically pointed Johnsonian periods, and that the speech of characters in Elizabethan plays was not almost entirely a series of exclamations over relatively ordinary matters. Yet it is our fault, and not the undergraduates'. If we deliberately alienate them by associating old-spelling texts with specialised scholarship which is over their heads, instead of offering it as the normal means of reading the literature of an earlier period—and a means that can be materially eased by a few typographical reforms—we alone, and our conservatism and pedantry, are to blame. The methods by which we can contrive that textual good money should drive out the bad are so obvious and so sane as to reflect seriously on our competence as teachers and as scholars if we reject this offered good and do not shape the editing of texts to our purposes instead of to the purposes of the publishers of textbooks and the laziness or timidity, but often only the inexperience, of our amateur academic editors.

NOTES

PAGE 2

1 This argument later appeared as 'Hamlet's "Sullied" or "Solid" Flesh: A Bibliographical Case-History', *Shakespeare Survey*, IX (1956), 44–8.

PAGE 3

1 'A Poem Nearly Anonymous', first printed in the *American Review* in 1933, and reprinted in *The World's Body* (1938). See Martin C. Battestin, 'John Crowe Ransom and *Lycidas:* A Reappraisal', *College English*, XVII (1956), 223–8, for a critical analysis of Ransom's position.

2 Kathleen Tillotson, reviewing Professor Spurgeon's *Shakespeare's Imagery and What It Tells Us*, wrote: 'Before appraising the results one should consider the ways in which the methods can be no more than approximate; for the margin of error, or variation, may be wide enough to lessen the scientific value which seems, at times, to be claimed for the results, though it need not lessen their value as accumulated impressions. The ultimate source of all data is the text. But what text? Professor Spurgeon has used Gollancz's *Larger Temple Shakespeare*, which generally gives the text of the Cambridge edition. It is a conservative text, but it has, for instance, about sixty emendations in *Antony and Cleopatra*, and many of these affect the images. In "*lackeying* the varying tide," and "an *autumn* 'twas That grew the more by reaping," the effective image-words are Theobald's; they may have been Shakespeare's words, but we cannot know, and so long as any case can be made for the Folio readings "lacking" and "Anthony," conclusions about "motiveless subservience" and "the perennial seasons" must be accepted cautiously. Again, in *1 Henry IV* "the plumed estridges that *wing* the wind" are Rowe's, and the context would imply that Shakespeare's "interest in the flight of birds" is not here in question. It would have been safer, perhaps, to follow the original texts or to omit or qualify images based on doubtful readings' (*Review of English Studies*, XII (1936), 458–9).

PAGE 4

1 Helge Kökeritz, *Shakespeare's Pronunciation* (1953). It is distressing to find in this book so little care for textual accuracy that all quotations are taken from the Folio without regard for the different forms of the primary Quarto texts in cases when the Folio is derived and unauthoritative. We have, thus, the anomaly that when forms are quoted from the good Quartos (the only true authoritative texts for most of the plays printed before the Folio), the special notation (Q) is affixed. Irregularities result from this practice, of course. For instance, if we are concerned with the forms that appear in the print nearest the manuscript and therefore *may* be Shakespearean, we may object to the listing under *syncopation* (p. 376) of *mockry M.N.D.* 2. 1. 111 from F instead of Q *mockery*. Here F has no authority, and the fact that the F compositor elided the *e* is not quite the point that Kökeritz had in mind when on p. 28 he remarked on the omission of a syncopated vowel: 'The poet himself rather than the typesetter is to blame for this carelessness....' Obviously a linguist who makes statements like this when innocent of information provided by compositor analysis is likely to be wrong about the agencies that produce the forms he is treating. For another instance, see the listing (p. 379) of *bach'ler M.N.D.* 2. 2. 59 from F instead of Q *batcheler*.

Doubtless there is as much significance in these variant forms as there is to his careful distinction (p. 376) between the spellings *watrie M.N.D.* 3. 1. 203 and *watry* 1. 1. 210, 2. 1. 162, when in fact all three are *watry* in authoritative Q and the *watrie* form is merely an unauthoritative F variant. Quotation of derived texts from the Folio thus results in constant distortion of spelling, elision, and so on; and the harm is not confined merely to forms in the quoted text that are not immediately under scrutiny.

Moreover, the habit of quoting from F leads to the reproduction of various unauthoritative F substantive errors for Q's substantive purity, as when (p. 116) he follows corrupt F *or* in *R.J.* 2. 4. 102 for correct Q2 *for*; or (p. 146) F's corrupt *to* in *R.J.* 1. 4. 20 for correct Q2 *so*; or (p. 147) F's *the* in *R.J.* 3. 2. 126 for Q2 *that*; or (p. 155) corrupt F *into* M.N.D. 2. 1. 191 for Q1 *vnto*.

The corrupt texts from which he often draws his quotations may affect the weight of the evidence supporting a linguistic argument. A typical case comes on p. 85 where Kökeritz is suggesting a pun on *woe-woo* and quotes F 'These times of *wo*, affoord no times to *wooe*' from *R.J.* 3. 4. 8. Then after remarking that 'The Q2 spellings are *woe* and *woo* respectively', he adds, 'This line should be compared with 3. 5. 120 where Juliet says:

"Ere he that should be Husband comes to *woe*,"

whose last word is spelled *wooe* in Q2.' But it must be obvious, surely, that the spellings in the derived F text of *Romeo and Juliet* cannot be utilised to show Shakespeare's intentions, which can only be determined by analysing the primary evidence of Q2 which was set from a manuscript commonly thought to be autograph. Hence the fact that F at 3. 5. 120 spells *woo* as *woe* is no evidence at all for a Shakespearean homonymic pun at 3. 4. 8 when at 3. 5. 120 Q2's spelling is *wooe*. Another instance comes on p. 83 when the pun Kökeritz is examining in *R.J.* 2. 4. 66–70 is materially aided by the sophisticated F text that he utilises, 'when the single sole of it is worne, the jeast may remain after the wearing, sole-singular', although the correct (but unmentioned) Shakespearean reading as found in Q2 is 'soly singular'. On p. 155, in relation to a pun in *M.N.D.* 2. 1. 192, the substantive Q1 reading (never mentioned) 'wodde, within this wood' is certainly more significant linguistically than the quoted unauthoritative F '*wood* within this *wood*' which has been sophisticated by a compositor.

Kökeritz's use of bad-quarto (memorially transmitted and corrupt) texts for the ostensible purpose of making points about Shakespeare's own practice is, of course, quite illogical, as when

(p. 104) he resorts to Q1 *Hamlet* 4. 3. 20 f., 'At supper, not where he is *eating*, but where he is *eaten*.' He then indicates that he believes Q1 to be a primary text, from which Q2 and F derive (and not a corrupt memorial report of the basic Q2–F text) when he adds, 'Perhaps the ambiguity of the pronunciation [ẹːtn] was the reason for changing *eating* into *eat(e)s* in Q2 and F'. If in 1953 linguists operate on the theory, discredited since the publication in 1941 of G. I. Duthie's *'Bad' Quarto of* Hamlet, that Q2 and F represent later texts than Q1, so that Shakespeare could have changed Q1 *is eating* to Q2–F *eats*, they are creating a merry world indeed. Similarly, the propriety of including under the heading 'An Index of Shakespeare's Rhymes' various jingles found only in the bad quartos is very doubtful. Care for the transmission of a text cannot be of no concern to linguistic inquiry.

IF *Hamlet* 4. 3. 20 above had been in an area in which Q1 can be demonstrated to have contaminated Q2, and IF Q2 is in fact physically in some manner the basic copy-text for F, then it could be argued that Q1 represents the true Shakespearean reading, corrupted in the printing of Q2 and thence passed on in error to F. But in Act IV there seems to be no such contamination as is found in Act I. This first-act contamination (not known to Kökeritz) affects the argument on p. 193 (see also p. 305), 'But the spellings *bettles* Q2 and *beckles* (Q) for *beetles Hamlet* 1. 4. 71 can hardly mean anything else than the short vowel [ẹ]'. Actually, this series means anything but the short vowel. In Q1 *beckles*, on the evidence, is an actor's faulty recollection (provided it is not a compositorial error), and there is every reason to suppose with Dover Wilson and Alice Walker that Q2 *bettles* owes its odd form to contamination from Q1. Hence no phonological assumptions that have any likelihood of being valid can be made in this case, and an imperfect notion of textual relationships has vitiated the linguistic conclusion.

Like Spurgeon, Kökeritz is on dangerous ground in taking his evidence for certain statements from the unauthoritative corrections of derived texts. Very likely F *checkring* is correct for *R.J.* 2. 3. 2, but is it advisable to use this compositorial emendation for Q2 *checking* as a valid example of authorial vowel syncopation (p. 381)?

2 Kökeritz's lack of information about bibliographical investigations leads him into such statements as (p. 22): 'The many phonetic spellings of one kind or another in the early Quartos and the First Folio need not, of course, reflect his [Shakespeare's] own usage, *though most of them undoubtedly do so* [my italics]. Even a copyist may have adhered pretty closely to Shakespeare's own spelling—at any rate, *not a single spelling can, even conjecturally, be attributed to such an intermediary*' (my italics). This rash statement ignores F. P. Wilson's study of the scribe Ralph Crane, whose characteristics can be detected in the Folio text of *The Merry Wives of Windsor*. It is directly controverted by the investigations of Dr Philip Williams into the Folio's variant spellings in such plays as *1 Henry VI* and *King John*. These show variant spellings in the work of the same compositor within each play, and they differ according to the *literary* divisions of the plays and must therefore be representative of the work of two different inscribers.

No bibliographer or working textual critic of Renaissance literature would subscribe without serious reservations to the optimism, based on insufficient or outdated evidence, that marks p. 23: 'These studies by Simpson, Darbishire, and Byrne prove Wyld (pp. 112 f.) to have been correct in laying down as his working hypothesis that the printers were "unlikely to introduce, of themselves, any considerable novelties in spelling"; that they were conservative and conventional; that they would be more likely to eliminate the "incorrect" spellings of the author's manuscript than introduce these themselves; and that consequently we are justified in regarding the outstanding linguistic features in printed literature of the period as really reflecting the individualities of the authors and not of the printers.'

3 Such as its failure to record the three examples in Shakespeare and the one in Dekker of the word *sally* meaning *sully*, although willing to record some other forms on a single suspect example.

Notes

4 A fascinating study of corruption in modern reading texts will be found in R. C. Bald, 'Editorial Problems—A Preliminary Survey', *Studies in Bibliography*, III (1950), 3–17. See also Gordon N. Ray, 'The Importance of Original Editions', *Nineteenth-Century English Books: Some Problems in Bibliography* (1952), pp. 8–12.

A typical case of reprints ignoring authorially corrected editions and returning to less authoritative texts is given by Stanley Godman in 'Lewis Carroll's Final Corrections to "Alice"', *Times Literary Supplement*, 2 May 1958, p. 248. For the 1897 editions of *Alice* and *Through the Looking-Glass* Carroll minutely revised the text. Mr Godman writes: 'The collation of the author's corrections with the editions of 1897 which I have made shows that, with two exceptions—one of them a regrettable oversight, the other owing perhaps to an understandable disagreement on the printer's part—his copious and sometimes finicking instructions were observed as scrupulously as they were made. A study of a representative selection of the editions that have appeared after his death shows, however, that the author's final intentions, as represented by the corrections in Mrs Stretton's copies and the 1897 editions based on them, have rarely been respected in their entirety. For example, the edition in Macmillan's "Sixpenny Series" (1898) and the Macmillan "Miniature" edition (1907) complied with only about a half of the amendments for the 1897 editions. Notable editions such as the Everyman (1929) and the Puffin (1946) ignore them altogether, the latter even reverting to the pre-1886 editions which contained only the first four lines of "'Tis the voice of the lobster" which was expanded in the edition of 1886 and the People's Edition of 1887.' It is clear from this and other evidence that the copy-texts for modern cheap reprints are likely to be most negligently selected. For various examples of corruptions, see Bruce Harkness, 'Bibliography and the Novelistic Fallacy' in *S.B.*, XII (1959), 59–73.

PAGE 5

1 *The Influence of Beaumont and Fletcher on Shakespeare* (1901), pp. 24 ff., noticed by Cyrus Hoy, 'The Shares of Fletcher and

his Collaborators in the Beaumont and Fletcher Canon (I)',
Studies in Bibliography, VIII (1956), 131, a thorough survey of
the problem using just such linguistic evidence but with some
care for the texts from which the evidence is drawn.

2 Carl J. Weber, 'American Editions of English Authors',
Nineteenth-Century English Books: Some Problems in Bibliography
(1952), pp. 31 ff. surveys the state of the text in early American
editions of Wordsworth, Thackeray, Fitzgerald, Hardy, and
Housman. Typical findings are as follows. In the 1802 James
Humphreys edition of Wordsworth published in Philadelphia,
the sixteen lines of 'Lines Written when Sailing in a Boat at
Evening' have been wrongly inserted as the opening lines of
'Lines written near Richmond, upon the Thames', with a com-
posite title of the publisher's invention, 'Lines written near
Richmond, upon the Thames, at Evening'. Although Thackeray
was most concerned about his illustrations for *Pendennis*, the contemporary authorised American edition by Harper omitted both
the frontispiece and the twenty-two full-page steel engravings.
Later, a pirated Lovell edition in New York included fifteen of
these but omitted all the smaller wood engravings. 'Some one
in the Harper office in New York struck out an entire page in
one chapter of Hardy's *Return of the Native*, solely to make the
book fit the format planned for the American edition; and after
Hardy had revised the text of this novel for the definitive London
edition of 1912, the American reader was still being offered the
debased New York product twenty-five years later. Most of the
pirates stole their own texts from just such debased, even though
"authorized", editions as the one here referred to, and the
likelihood that any librarian or scholar or collector would, in
buying an American copy, get the author's approved text was
very small, as long as the lack of international copyright per-
mitted the continuance of the chaotic conditions here described.
...Not until 1928 could any American librarian be *sure* that if
he bought a copy of *Tess* from the American publisher, he would
get the text as approved by the novelist himself.' Hardy's *Wood-
landers* by 1926 had been printed in at least thirty American

editions, all retaining the wording of the original London seriali-
sation in *Macmillan's Magazine*. But even before the first book
publication in England, Hardy had found the magazine text
unsatisfactory and had revised it, and he made additional revisions for the second edition. In 1895, in preparation for the
Uniform Edition of his writings, he once more revised the text,
and finally—for the fourth time—for the 1912 London edition.
Yet not until 1928 did an American edition appear (save in the
reissued sheets of the expensive set of his entire works) with the
text in its definitive state, or in a state representing *any* of the
previous revisions. These early unrevised texts are still, of course,
prominent on library shelves in the United States. After various
other examples, the inevitable conclusion is drawn: 'The student
of nineteenth-century English literature has only one safe rule
to follow: if he is working with an American edition of his
author, nothing can be taken for granted....The wise man...
will *know* his American edition before he goes far with it. He will
trust it as he would a rattlesnake. He will neither quote from it,
nor rely on conclusions drawn from it, until he has compared
it, word for word, with the present English edition, or has
assured himself that the English author saw and approved of
what his American publisher put into print for him. This has,
unfortunately, *not* been the practice of all American critics,
scholars, bibliographers, and others who have worked with the
books of English authors. They have thus opened the door to
unsound judgments, to inaccurate quotations, to misleading
conclusions, and to the perpetuation of faulty texts.'

That the practice is not confined merely to nineteenth-century
texts may be seen in an example kindly furnished me by
Mr Frederick Woods, who is proposing a bibliography of Sir
Winston Churchill. Galleys of *The Second World War* were
made up from the typescript, but successive stages of revision
were given to the galleys, so heavy as to amount to actual re-
writing in proof. At a certain stage in the process the American
publisher is reputed to have grown tired of waiting for further
textual revisions and revised maps and to have sent the book to

press. On the contrary, the English publisher waited for the further corrections and several months after the appearance of the first American edition published a different and certainly more authoritative text in the first English edition.

This is an extreme example, of course, but in many minor ways texts may differ between the two countries. I recall my own sense of shock on finding that Heinemann had religiously substituted 'petrol' for 'gas' or 'gasoline', even in the speech of the American characters where it was singularly inappropriate, when in 1952 my wife's novel *The Sign of Jonah* was reprinted in England. Bruce Harkness, 'Bibliography and the Novelistic Fallacy', *Studies in Bibliography*, XII (1959), should be consulted for further examples of misleading prose-fiction texts.

PAGE 6

1 'Editorial Problems', *Studies in Bibliography*, III (1950), 5.

PAGE 9

1 Matthew Bruccoli, 'A Collation of F. Scott Fitzgerald's *This Side of Paradise*', *Studies in Bibliography*, IX (1957), 263-5. A total of thirty-one changes were made in the original plates between 1920 and 1954: 'corrections of misspelled references to books and authors (10); corrections of misspellings of names and places (5); other corrections in spelling and usage (6); corrections of errors involving careless proof-reading (3); corrections of miscellaneous errors (3); and revisions of non-errors (4)'. Although the literary critic will be most concerned with the final category, the others are of some account, as Edmund Wilson noticed, when he wrote: 'It is not only full of bogus ideas and faked literary references but it is full of English words misused with the most reckless abandon.' Some but not all of these original faults were concealed by the correction of the plates.

The analysis of a modern author's linguistic habits by studying the changes made in different printings of his books is still a rare pursuit, but interesting results may follow. The correction of faulty grammar in the second printing of Sherwood Anderson's novel *Winesburg, Ohio* as a result of a caustic newspaper review is interesting in its own right; and in addition it established for collectors the order of the first two printings, which—on evidence that collectors usually get bilked by—had been confused. See William L. Phillips, 'The First Printing of Sherwood Anderson's *Winesburg, Ohio*', *Studies in Bibliography*, IV (1951), 211–13.

2 *Times Literary Supplement*, 20 May 1949, p. 329; quoted by Bald, *op. cit.* III, 4.

PAGE 10

1 In each case the exact nature of the Folio printer's copy is still in dispute. Until this is demonstrated once and for all, the authority of some of the Folio variants (or concurrences) cannot be determined.

PAGE 11

1 This illustration is drawn from an article by the Yeats Variorum editor, Russel K. Alspach, 'Some Textual Problems in Yeats', *Studies in Bibliography*, IX (1957), 51–67, which contains many more significant examples.

PAGE 12

1 Linton Massey, 'Notes on the Unrevised Galleys of Faulkner's *Sanctuary*', *Studies in Bibliography*, VIII (1956), 195–208. The structure of the novel was completely altered, and the original hero demoted to a quite minor role. In Mr Massey's words, 'Faulkner altered the entire focus and meaning of the book; he clarified the obscure passages where ambiguity was not an asset; he amplified those portions requiring emendation; he gave the novel a climax; and he freed it from its bonds of previous servitude to an earlier book'.

PAGE 13

1 A study of this manuscript will be found in Bowers, 'The Earliest Manuscript of Whitman's "Passage to India" and its Notebook', *Bulletin of the New York Library*, LXI (1957), 319–52, which forms a preface to the account of the later Harvard manu-

script and its proofs in 'The Manuscript of Whitman's "Passage to India"', *Modern Philology*, LI (1953), 102–17. Reference may also be made to the critical value of the evidence for stages of composition and revision in two other Whitman manuscripts, 'The Manuscript of Walt Whitman's "A Carol of Harvest, for 1867"', *Modern Philology*, LII (1954), 29–51; and 'The Manuscripts of Whitman's "Song of the Redwood Tree"', *Papers of the Bibliographical Society of America*, L (1956), 53–85.

PAGE 16

1 The complexities of this process, and its importance for understanding the operation of an author's mind as he shapes his work, contrast with what I must regard as the narrowness of such a passage as this, quoted by R. C. Bald from Wellek and Warren: 'If we examine drafts, rejections, exclusions, and cuts, we conclude them not, finally, necessary to an understanding of the finished work or to a judgment upon it. Their interest is that of any alternative, i.e., they may set into relief the qualities of the final text. But the same end may very well be achieved by devising for ourselves alternatives, whether or not they have actually passed through the author's mind' (*Theory of Literature*, p. 86). The quotation comes as a footnote to Professor Bald's own position: 'No one, I fancy, will dispute the fact that one of the functions of a definitive edition is to illuminate as much as possible the origin and development of the work edited. Every student of the Romantic Period, for instance, knows something of the fascinating struggle for artistic perfection revealed by Keats's manuscripts, or of the information about the development of Wordsworth's thought and art furnished by the new Oxford edition.'

But editorial duty aside, if we take such a test case as David Hayman's 'From *Finnegans Wake*: A Sentence in Progress', *PMLA*, LXXIII (1958), 136–54, a fascinating analysis of the growth in meaning of a single sentence, it is difficult to hold that only the finished result is of critical interest for the explication of a work or of any of its parts. Most great works contain some

mystery, some levels of allusiveness that may easily be overlooked
or even misunderstood, although, as with Joyce, the evidence for
their growth will clarify and explain. The school of criticism
represented by Messrs Wellek and Warren is confident that the
single perspicuous critic, face to face with the work in isolation,
requires no aids to understanding, such as early drafts fixing the
stages of growth. This may well be true if the critic (as they seem
to do) searches the drafts only for rejected or imperfect variants
which serve to highlight the superior values of the finished product. If one takes it that the end result is perfect, of course the
critic can himself contrive alternatives that will serve to show the
superiority of the final form. But if the critic is like Dr Hayman,
for example, and is endeavouring to demonstrate on the evidence
of early drafts what the meaning of the end result must be, he is
concerned with a method of criticism quite different from that
pursued by Wellek and Warren, and one with far different ideals.
That unaided critical speculation about meaning in the New
Critical manner of explication must always fail in its full objective
is adroitly argued by W. Y. Tindall in 'The Criticism of Fiction',
The Texas Quarterly, I (1958), 101–11, especially on p. 109.

2 Information in this chapter about Eliot's text comes, unless
otherwise stated, from Robert L. Beare, 'Notes on the Text
of T. S. Eliot: Variants from Russell Square', *Studies in Bibliography*, IX (1957), 21–49, which is packed with interesting
examples.

PAGE 19

1 Matthew J. Bruccoli, 'Textual Variants in Sinclair Lewis's
Babbitt', *Studies in Bibliography*, XI (1958), 263–8.

PAGE 20

1 A number of examples exposed by the Hinman Collating
Machine will be found in Matthew J. Bruccoli, *Notes on the
Cabell Collections at the University of Virginia* (James Branch
Cabell: A Bibliography, Part II; University of Virginia Press,
1957). See especially the entry for *Jurgen*.

Notes

PAGE 22

1 Donald F. Bond, 'The First Printing of the *Spectator*', *Modern Philology*, XLVII (1950), 164–77.

2 'The Shares of Fletcher and his Collaborators in the Beaumont and Fletcher Canon', *Studies in Bibliography*, VIII (1956), 129–46 (see especially pp. 137–42); *S.B.*, IX (1957), 143–62 (see especially pp. 144–5); *S.B.*, XI (1958), 85–106, and later volumes.

3 'Printer's Copy for *The Two Noble Kinsmen*', *Studies in Bibliography*, XI (1958), 61–84.

PAGE 23

1 *The Dramatic Works of Thomas Dekker*, vol. III (1958).

PAGE 25

1 Donald F. Bond, 'The Text of the *Spectator*', *Studies in Bibliography*, V (1952), 109–28.

PAGE 26

1 *The Early Collected Editions of Shelley's Poems: A Study in the History and Transmission of the Printed Text.* The pertinent details are excerpted in Dr Taylor's 'The Errata Leaf to Shelley's *Posthumous Poems* and some Surprising Relationships between the Earliest Collected Editions', *PMLA*, LXX (1955), 408–16.

PAGE 27

1 Matthew J. Bruccoli, 'Textual Variants in Sinclair Lewis's *Babbitt*', *Studies in Bibliography*, XI (1958), 263–8.

PAGE 28

1 'An Unwritten Book' in *The Permanence of Yeats*, ed. James Hall and Martin Steinmann (1950), pp. 327–8, reprinted from *The Southern Review*, VII (1942), 488–90.

PAGE 30

1 See John W. Nichol, 'Melville's "Soiled" Fish of the Sea', *American Literature*, XXI (1949), 338–9. Dr Nichol comments, 'It is interesting to note that the change in this case does not invalidate the general critical position arrived at by Matthiessen;

it merely weakens his specific example. However, such a textual slip could, in the proper context, have promulgated an entirely false conception.'

2   The discussion was initiated by the following communication from R. A. Auty (*T.L.S.* 11 August 1950, p. 50): 'I find my efforts to read modern poetry made very difficult by never being certain what a poet wrote. Sometimes this may not matter very much, but in a poem like "Byzantium" every word is supposed to count. I had become used to

> A starlit or a moonlit dome disdains
> All that man is

when I came upon "distains" in Miss Gwendolyn Murphy's *The Modern Poet*. She informed me that she nearly always took the text for her anthology from the first printing, and that "distains" appeared in the original Irish edition, and that "disdains" crept into Macmillan's first printing and has persisted ever since. She thinks, and I agree, that "distains" is so much the better that it surely must be right.

'On asking Messrs Macmillan about the matter I am told that the suggestion has been made to them before. "We consulted Mrs Yeats about it. As she did not reply we took it that no alteration in the present text was necessary. We do not possess a copy of the first printing of this poem, and can only say that the author saw it several times in proof in various forms, and that he did not alter "disdains".

'This does not make me feel any more hopeful. If literature lessons, examinations and criticism are based on what a poet did not write then the whole thing becomes more of a dishonest game than they already are.'

Thereupon the reading was inconclusively debated, and other errors in Yeats's text noticed by Gwendolyn Murphy, Richard Murphy, Maurice Craig, Peter Ure, Dennis Silk, John Christopherson, Vernon Watkins, and Bonamy Dobrée on 25 August, p. 533; 1 September, p. 549; 8 September, p. 565; 15 September, p. 581; 22 September, p. 597; 3 November, p. 693, respectively.

Notes

In this general connection one may cite a recent article that attempts to analyse why critics generally prefer the corrupt reading of a metaphor to the author's true reading: see Walker Percy, 'Metaphor as Mistake', *The Sewanee Review*, LXVI (1958), 79–99.

PAGE 33

1 William H. Marshall, 'The Text of T. S. Eliot's "Gerontion"', *Studies in Bibliography*, IV (1951), 213–17.

PAGE 34

1 I am indebted to Professor Oscar Maurer in the University of Texas for the following illustrative note: 'The two editions of James Joyce's *Ulysses* commonly read in America are the Random House edition, published in 1934 soon after the decision (December 1933) by Judge Woolsey which made its publication legal in the United States, and the Modern Library edition, which was from the same plates in the same year. The Modern Library "Giant" has been reprinted several times: later printings, after Joyce's death, include a notice of copyright by Nora Joyce (1942, 1946).

'All the copies I have seen have a misprint on p. 76 which has the effect of defeating the author's purpose. Line 5 of the letter received by Leopold Bloom from his unknown correspondent Martha Clifford should read, "I do not like that other world" (a deliberate error on Joyce's part). The American editions correct this to, 'that other word''—an alteration which makes meaningless two later passages in the novel. When Bloom replies to the letter (p. 275) he meditates, "Other world she wrote." Again on the beach after the Gerty MacDowell scene (p. 375) the phrase recurs, "What is the meaning of that other world."

'A comparison with the Paris editions (Shakespeare and Co., 1922, etc.) will show that Joyce originally wrote "world". The significance of the slip in Bloom's later thoughts about it, and its suggestiveness in the work of a verbally sensitive writer (who was also interested in the psychological meaning of errors in speech—e.g. Bloom's "wife's admirers" for "wife's advisers",

p. 307) show the importance of a valid text, especially in widely circulated editions like the Modern Library *Ulysses*.'

James F. Spoerri, 'The Odyssey Press Edition of James Joyce's *Ulysses*', *Papers of the Bibliographical Society of America*, L (1956), 195–8, contributes a list of other misprints in the course of transmission.

2 'Henry James Reprints', *Times Literary Supplement*, 5 February 1949, p. 96. Notice is taken that James extensively revised his works for the definitive New York edition of 1907–9, and for some time thereafter all reprints—protected by copyright—were based on this revision. In 1941 republishing became possible for anyone willing to pay the statutory royalty fee; but it was not until after the war that Rupert Hart-Davis reprinted the earlier versions of the text and John Lehmann the revised forms. Commenting on Hart-Davis's defence of his position, the *T.L.S.* writer remarks: 'If this is arguable of the stories of the middle years, comparatively lightly revised after a comparatively short interval, then *a fortiori* to read the stories that made James's name in 1875–80—*Roderick Hudson*, *The American*, *Daisy Miller*, *Four Meetings*, *Madame de Mauves*, *The Portrait of a Lady*—to read these in texts that he sophisticated after thirty years is to make a mockery of "development" and to deaden the impact of a fresh mind upon a receptive generation.'

He then points out that in *The Great Tradition*, F. R. Leavis 'suggests that there is danger in centring critical attention upon James's development, the danger of overlooking "the striking measure of achievement that marks even the opening phase of his career"—that marks, for example, James's "first attempt at a novel, *Roderick Hudson* (1874)"'. Dr Leavis sees the strong influence of Dickens on *Roderick Hudson*, and quotes as an example the passage describing the visit of Mr Leavenworth to Hudson's studio in Rome. The only difficulty is that the text of the quoted passage supposedly illustrating James's manner in 1874 comes from the greatly revised edition of 1907; and when the corresponding text from the first book edition in 1876 is placed beside it, one can see that Dickens's influence came in the

Notes

1907 revision and was not present, as Leavis believed, in the original writing. The *T.L.S.* writer was justified, therefore, in his wintry summation: 'When after having quoted this [the 1907 text of *Roderick Hudson*], Mr Leavis "jumps forward a dozen years" to seek the influence of Dickens in *The Bostonians* (1886), he is really jumping backward a score. So much for the danger of paying too much attention to development'—and, one may add, too little attention to text.

PAGE 35

1 Bowers, *Whitman's Manuscripts: Leaves of Grass* (1860) (1955). The introduction to this edition, pp. xxiii–lxxiv, holds the facts upon which the narrative of this lecture is based. For various critical suggestions I am indebted to Dr W. Stephen Sanderlin's unpublished University of Virginia dissertation, *The Growth of Leaves of Grass 1856–1860*.

PAGE 37

1 'An Essay on *Leaves of Grass*', in *Leaves of Grass One Hundred Years After*, ed. Milton Hindus (1955), p. 23.

PAGE 71

1 By 'extended too far' I mean extended beyond the area of such simple confusion as the Q2 misreading *comiration* of what, from *Romeo and Juliet* Q1, we may accept as manuscript *coniuration*. No one can deny the usefulness of palaeographical evidence in a restricted area. The method only becomes dangerous when it is utilised as the *only* method (as by Sisson), when it is thought to have more value as evidence than bibliographical assumptions, and when it begins to operate on the fringes of probability (as it always will when taken to be the only emendatory method that has a basis in precise physical evidence). In my opinion, these three objections serve to decrease the usefulness of C. J. Sisson's *New Readings in Shakespeare*, 2 vols. (Shakespeare Problem Series, VIII [1956]).

2 *Shakespeare Quarterly*, VIII (1957), 104–7.

Notes

PAGE 77

1 'The Compositors of *Hamlet* Q2 and *The Merchant of Venice*', *Studies in Bibliography*, VII (1955), 17–40; see also Paul. L. Cantrell and George Walton Williams, 'Roberts' Compositors in *Titus Andronicus* Q2', *S.B.*, VIII (1956), 27–38.

PAGE 79

1 The first announcement of the use of identified types as bibliographical evidence was made by Dr Charlton Hinman in 'Cast-Off Copy for the First Folio of Shakespeare', *Shakespeare Quarterly*, VI (1955), 259–73; followed by 'The Prentice Hand in the Tragedies of the Shakespeare First Folio: Compositor E', *Studies in Bibliography*, IX (1957), 3–20. Full information is expected in a monograph now in preparation on the printing of the First Folio.

2 Notably George Walton Williams, 'Setting by Formes in Quarto Printing', *Studies in Bibliography*, XI (1958), 39–53. More information will be found in Robert K. Turner, 'The Composition of *The Insatiate Countess*, Q2', in *S.B.*, XII (1959).
'Setting by formes' means, in quarto, that the type-pages of a sheet were not set in order, as 1, 1^v, 2, 2^v, 3, 3^v, 4, and 4^v, but instead in selected order as a forme, i.e. either 1^v, 2, 3^v, 4 and then 1, 2^v, 3, 4^v, or the reverse. In the Shakespeare First Folio, when a quire was set simultaneously by two workmen, compositor A might set p. 6 while compositor B set p. 7 (to use pagination numbers for this example), then A would proceed to p. 5 and B to p. 8, then A to p. 4 and B to p. 9, until A came to p. 1 and B to p. 12. Then in the next gathering B would start with p. 18 and A with p. 19, B would proceed to p. 17 and A to p. 20, and so on, until the quire was completed with B setting p. 13 and A setting p. 24, the outer forme of the outermost sheet. For compositors to work in this manner, setting by formes, the printer's copy must be 'cast off' and marked with the amount of material estimated for each page; and the compositors must observe this marking scrupulously. When type is set by formes (i.e. the type-pages necessary to print one side of a sheet of

paper), less type is required and in some respects presswork is speeded at the start. Thus in quarto a forme is ready for the press after the interval required for the composition of only four type-pages instead of the seven required to complete the inner forme if pages are set in order. In the First Folio, when *A* set p. 6 and *B* p. 7, the inner forme of the inmost sheet of the quire was ready for the press after the setting of only two pages, instead of the seven required if setting had been seriatim. This inner forme was then perfected with pp. 5 and 8 comprising the outer forme. Since a compositor perforce adjusted his material to predetermined limits for each page when setting by formes, important textual consequences may result from the mechanical process of printing when the casting-off had not been completely accurate and he was forced to compress his material, or to expand it, to fit the pre-assigned space.

PAGE 80

1 'A Note on *Coriolanus*', *J. Q. Adams Memorial Studies* (1948), 239–52.

PAGE 82

1 'Compositor Determination and Other Problems', *Studies in Bibliography*, VII (1955), 9–10.

2 'New Approaches to Textual Problems in Shakespeare', *Studies in Bibliography*, VIII (1956), 3–14.

PAGE 85

1 'The Textual Relation of Q2 to Q1 *Hamlet*', *Studies in Bibliography*, VIII (1956), 39–66.

PAGE 87

1 P. L. Cantrell and G. W. Williams, 'The Printing of the Second Quarto of *Romeo and Juliet* (1599)', *Studies in Bibliography*, IX (1957), 107–28; see also Richard Hosley, 'Quarto Copy for Q2 *Romeo and Juliet*', *S.B.*, IX, 129–41. These correct J. Dover Wilson in the New Cambridge *Romeo and Juliet* and

in 'The New Way with Shakespeare's Texts: II. Recent Work on the Text of *Romeo and Juliet*', *Shakespeare Survey*, VIII (1955), 81–99.

PAGE 96

1 J. K. Walton, *The Copy for the Folio Text of Richard III* (Auckland University College, Monograph Series, no. 1, 1955); Andrew S. Cairncross, 'Coincidental Variants in *Richard III*', *The Library*, 5th ser. XII (1957), 187–90; but chiefly 'The Quartos and the Folio Text of *Richard III*', *Review of English Studies*, n.s. VIII (1957), 225–33.

PAGE 109

1 The relation of any such pattern (if it developed) to the two compositors' division of Q2, or to the three compositors' division of F, would be highly significant, since no pattern that did not ignore bibliographical divisions of either text could be logically related to the underlying printer's copy unless patterns of error directly related to the separate compositors could be established.

PAGE 110

1 Such studies as 'The Folio Text of *1 Henry IV*', *Studies in Bibliography*, VI (1954), 45–59; 'Collateral Substantive Texts (with special reference to *Hamlet*)', *S.B.*, VII (1955), 51–67; 'Some Editorial Principles (with special reference to *Henry V*)', *S.B.*, VIII (1956), 95–111.

PAGE 112

1 From M. A. Shaaber's searching review in *Shakespeare Quarterly*, VIII (1957), 104–7. Professor Shaaber rightly sees that 'Not only his new readings but his defense of the original text or of some emendation often rests on the *cursus litterarum*'. This narrow base for textual criticism obviously will not support all the readings that must be chosen from multiple authority or the emendations that must be made, and hence Sisson is led into the old-fashioned sort of eclecticism—mere personal choice— without regard for the facts of textual transmission. This

Notes

Shaaber sees very clearly: 'Mr Sisson tends to consider each crux in isolation and to weigh every variety of argument pro and con in reaching a decision. From time to time he says something like "I resort to an eclectic reading" (II, 110) or "it is indeed difficult to avoid a stylistic eclecticism in this play" (II, 88). For example, in the first reading in *Hamlet* which he discusses, he protests against giving 1. 1. 21 to Marcellus (Q1, F) rather than Horatio (Q2), but he does not raise the question of the authority of the several texts and is apparently convinced by the fact that "The speech is quite inappropriate to Marcellus".' It is this lack of principle that troubles Professor Shaaber, as it troubles other good scholars. But the answer is not the extreme of denying the validity of eclecticism and for the sake of principle embracing the equally faulty textual method of the 'best' text and all that this implies (see p. 121 n. 1 below). Instead, as this review does not go on to point out, the method of modern bibliographical logic can be used to limit the area in which eclecticism can operate and to provide a reasonable basis for most eclectic choices. Then when—as will sometimes be necessary—the pure critical judgement must be trusted in cases where textual bibliography cannot provide the required evidence, or suggest the probability, the editor (and his reader) knows which discipline he is favouring and makes his choice on grounds that are clear-cut, not a confusion of two disciplines. Only by such a distinction can a reader ever know where he stands.

PAGE 119
1 *The Editorial Problem in Shakespeare* (2nd ed. 1951), p. l.

PAGE 121
1 *Ibid.* p. xxviii: 'Now it appears to me that so long as we assert that the aim of a critical edition is to attain as nearly as possible to the words of the author (as laid down in Rule 1) we have no choice but to accept the eclectic principle (which in fact follows logically from it) whatever textual uncertainties this may involve, since the opposite conservative principle only attains certainty

(if it does attain it) at the cost of critical freedom in pursuit of our declared object.'

2 *Ibid.* p. liv n. 2. 3 *Ibid.* pp. xxviii ff.

PAGE 122

1 *The Dramatic Works of Thomas Dekker*, II (1955), 3–19. For another case see also pp. 231–52 devoted to an analysis of the variable authority of the readings in the second edition of *The Magnificent Entertainment*.

PAGE 128

1 It is difficult to generalise in this matter, owing to the variation to be expected between compositors and the paucity of recovered information we possess at this time. The one case in which I have personal knowledge from investigation did not turn out too promisingly on the whole. Although it was possible to assign authorship of the scenes of *The Virgin Martyr* (1622) as Massinger's or Dekker's on a few orthographical characteristics that had slipped through the compositor, and even to infer at least one scene in which Dekker had rewritten Massinger's original, the positive evidence for Massinger was less throughout than for Dekker. In fact, so few of Massinger's distinctive characteristics came through, and the result bore so little relation to the characteristics of Massinger's own manuscript of the play *Believe As You List*, as to lead to some question whether—against apparent probability—the underlying printer's copy for these scenes had indeed been a Massinger holograph, as there had been every reason to expect. Such an experience, and with a play in which we should have expected authorial foul papers from both writers, gives a bibliographer cold shivers when he hears a linguist confidently pronounce the vast majority of occasional spellings in Shakespeare's printed texts to be undoubtedly authorial. We do not as yet even begin to have the facts upon which any real judgement can be made. All we can say is that we know (*a*) many compositors had a very few invariable characteristics that they regularly imposed upon their copy regardless of its nature; (*b*) some success has attended investiga-

tions into the influence of authorial characteristics on compositors. But the authorial orthographic details that penetrate the veil of print, in these test cases, have not proved so numerous as to give bibliographers complete confidence in the authorial characteristics that may be preserved in any given print, although some, of course, are to be anticipated (especially if the print is nearly contemporary with the manuscript).

2 The causes of variance, in different prints, of the compositorial characteristics that serve as differentia in any one print are most puzzling and not wholly to be explained by the possible effect of copy-spellings. Not much information is available about this matter, but one may consult for some statistics John Russell Brown, 'The Compositors of *Hamlet* Q2 and *The Merchant of Venice*', *Studies in Bibliography*, VII (1955), 17 ff.; and also the unpublished University of Virginia dissertations by George Walton Williams on *Romeo and Juliet* and by Robert K. Turner on *The Maid's Tragedy*, available on microfilm.

PAGE 129

1 That printing-house rules existed and were followed by Elizabethan compositors, or that (if they existed and were followed) they were extensive enough to obscure orthographical characteristics of the copy, let alone individual compositorial characteristics, is a proposition in which I have no faith. I should like to see the evidence for the assertion that is sometimes made to this effect. However, here and there one comes upon some possible case of an individual proof-reader who may be trying to impose his own standards on a compositor. For instance, in Dekker's *Wonder of a Kingdom* (1636) inner forme A (containing the start of the text) was revised three times before the proof-reader decided he had got it right. Thereafter, when press-variants appear they are so skimpy as to suggest that the proof-reader had had a word with the compositor after sheet A. (But we must not assume that this was the first book set in this shop by the compositor!) In another possible case, the first edition of Dryden's *Wild Gallant* (1669) had seen a relatively indifferent

use of *then* or of *than* for the conjunction *than*; but the second edition in the same year used the *than* form invariably, and the one time the compositor slipped and followed his first-edition copy in using *then*, the proof-reader caught him up and changed the spelling in the correction of the forme. Yet this second edition with its very different orthographical practice was set in the very same shop as the first. Whether the rigour in using the *than* spelling in Q2 was characteristic of the compositor I do not know; but it is at least suggestive that the proof-reader spotted the variant spelling the one time (so far as extensive collation discloses) that it appeared. Hence it may be that the proof-reader in this matter insisted on the *than* spelling early in the typesetting and saw to it that the compositor followed his wishes. However, we cannot on the evidence of the second edition argue that Thomas Newcombe's printing-house had a 'rule' about this usage, especially when we consider the largely indifferent spelling of the first edition, also set in Newcombe's shop only a short time before. If one is acquainted with the text of an Elizabethan play only in its corrected formes, doubtless one may be misled about some features of quasi-uniformity that could be imposed by a strongminded proof-reader such as the one who read Chettle's *Hoffman* (1631) or the one who read Dekker's *Match Me in London* (1631). But statistically the interference is quite minor; and its very existence, indeed, argues against the existence of shop rules if they were so frequently violated by the compositors. It is interesting to observe that despite the constant attentions of the printing-house reader to the proofs of *Match Me*, the compositor gives no evidence of improvement, or prior consideration to the kind of errors the proof-reader attempted to correct, as he sets sheet after sheet up to the very end.

PAGE 130

1   *Editorial Problem*, pp. li–lii.

PAGE 131

1   *Ibid.* p. li. Greg continues: 'To print *banquet* for *banket*, *fathom* for *fadom*, *lantern* for *lanthorn*, *murder* for *murther*, *mush-*

room for mushrump, orphan for *orphant, perfect* for *parfit, port-cullis* for *perculace, tattered* for *tottered, vile* for *vild, wreck* for *wrack*, and so on, and so on, is sheer perversion.'

2 An instance would be *murther* for *murder*, retained by both New Arden and New Yale editors on formal or on assumed pro-nunciation grounds. Yet every Elizabethan textual critic is accustomed to quite random intermixture of these two spellings within the same text where, certainly, no distinction could be intended, or could be significant. See Alice Walker, 'Com-positor Determination and Other Problems in Shakespearian Texts', *Studies in Bibliography*, VII (1955), 4 and fn.: 'Among textual critics, though wiser heads have never supposed that the spelling of printed books was the author's (the Old Cambridge editors, for instance, rejected the idea of an old spelling Shake-speare on this account), there is even yet a great deal of muddled thinking. Spellings of one writer are compared with those of another on the evidence of different dates from different printing houses [fn. 1: H. T. Price, for instance, in *English Institute Essays 1947* (1948), 143–58] and the vagaries of compositors are being erratically introduced into modernised texts of Shakespeare [fn. 2: I have remarked on this in a recent review of the New Arden *Titus Andronicus*. It is the general policy of the new series "to preserve all older forms that are more than variant spellings"—a policy which has not, I suspect, been seen in relation to logical linguistic conclusions. When Muir, for instance, in the New Arden *Lear*, followed the Folio's "murther", what was he reproducing—the compositor's spelling or a scribal alteration of the Q1 spelling on the authority of the *Lear* prompt-book? If it was a prompt-book spelling, was it Shakespeare's? Further, if consonant variants, like "murther" and "vild", are preserved, why not the vowel variants in "show" and "shew", "blood" and "bloud"? Why not the common "alablaster" or "abhomin-able" and (contrariwise), in early texts, "clime" for "climb" or "limmes" for "limbs"? Muir went so far as to reproduce Compositor *B*'s arbitrary distinctions between -'d and -ed of weak preterites and past participles in prose. But what will

happen in the New Arden *As You Like It* where there are two compositors favouring different conventions? Modern English is one thing; the habits of the compositors of Shakespearian texts are quite another, and the arbitrary preservation of a selection of the latter has no linguistic principles behind it.]'

3   The plain facts of the matter are, we do not yet have satisfactory information to serve in many cases as the ground for decision. Greg remarks: 'Today a standard orthography masks quite a wide divergence of pronunciation even among people of the same local and social surroundings. In Shakespeare's day a writer's individualities of speech reflected themselves naturally in his spelling, and to alter his spelling is to destroy a clue to his language. There is always a difficulty in distinguishing between what are really different phonetic forms and what are mere arbitrary variations of spelling. How far in Elizabethan times did the spellings *dance* and *daunce* reflect any difference or fluctuation of pronunciation? Which is only to say that, whether in itself normalization is desirable or not, our present philological equipment is inadequate to the task. This anyhow rules it out as a practical expedient' (*Editorial Problem*, p. li). Earlier linguists (and some still even today, as in the recent discussions of Shakespeare by Partridge and Kökeritz) were in the habit of drawing examples for phonological discussion from printed texts on the innocent assumption that these texts could be trusted to mirror with major faithfulness the author's characteristics. Greater sophistication has led other scholars to select only manuscripts, the more ingenuous the better, as superior authority to prints. But, as I understand it, the most advanced linguists now recognise that holograph needs disentangling from scribal manuscripts (which are no better than prints), that schooling may have influenced spelling in Elizabethan times though not necessarily pronunciation, and hence that many factors not previously enough considered may enter into the complex question how far orthography actually may represent phonology. When among the giants so much about Elizabethan pronunciation is still in controversy, it is certainly unreasonable to invite the editor of

a modernised text to outwit the experts by deciding in a long series of examples whether orthographical variation is or is not so significant as to be worth retaining.

4 In a thoughtful review of the New Arden *Titus Andronicus*, Greg pointed out some of the inconsistencies of selection: 'While necessarily modernizing spelling, he [the editor] retains what he regards as distinct early forms, like *murther*, *banket*, and *vild*, and would, I suppose, have kept *fadom* had it occurred. At the same time he refuses *tortering*, and would, I suppose, reject *venter*; what would he do with the well authenticated form *totter* for *tatter*? As he says, consistency is hardly attainable, and it is difficult to draw the line. He very sensibly refuses to reduce *and* to *an* when it means *if*, but how when the original reads *an't* or *an if*, both of which occur in the Folio': *Modern Language Review*, XLIX (1954), 362; quoted, with other pertinent evidence, by Arthur Brown, 'Editorial Problems in Shakespeare: Semi-Popular Editions', *Studies in Bibliography*, VIII (1956), 19.

PAGE 132

1 Alice Walker writes authoritatively in 'Some Editorial Principles (with special reference to *Henry V*)', *Studies in Bibliography*, VIII (1956), 109: 'Obviously if he [an editor] is not a phonologist he is severely handicapped, since it is one thing for an old spelling editor to preserve all copy-text spellings which are not errors but a very different matter to preserve a selection of old spellings and to justify one's choice. An old spelling editor, for instance, would not hesitate over "strooke" (p.p.) in the above list. Even if he cannot give a phonological account of the spelling, he will have seen it often enough. But what must the partially modernising editor do about it? He has to interpret the spelling in terms of the pronunciation related, by one means or another, to the O.E. strong verb which, by normal sound development, would have resulted in "strike", "stroke" (pret.), "stricken", and he must canvas the possibility of analogy (with, for instance, "stick", "stuck") or dialectal influence (as suggested by Kökeritz) before he can decide whether "strooke" indicated a different sound from "struck", which was in process of superseding it. An old spelling editor is concerned with old *spelling*; partial modernisation involves discrimination between one spelling and another on a *phonological* basis. This is a far more tricky business, which must inevitably lead to arbitrary measures, since even experts may often be put to it to decide what sounds some spellings represent; nor will experts always agree [fn: Thus Kökeritz (p. 176) seems inclined to think that Shakespeare's rhymes of "chaste", "haste", "taste", and "waste" with "blast", "fast", "last", etc. were eye rhymes, though citing Bulloker and later evidence for a pronunciation going back to M.E. ă in the former group of words. Since some compositors (e.g. Roberts's) almost invariably used the short spellings ("chast" etc.) and others (e.g. Simmes's) had as firm a preference for the long spellings, the partially modernising editor has to decide whether to follow Shakespeare's compositors' spellings or act on Kökeritz's conclusion that Shakespeare used the obsolescent pronunciation (from M.E. ă) in rhymes and some puns].'

The significant conclusion of this argument (pp. 109–11) should be referred to by an interested reader. This last quotation is only a small part of an important statement: 'It has often been said that "Shakespeare" has one spelling oftener than another, as if the spelling of printed books was the author's, and the antiquarian zeal for partial modernisation is perhaps prompted by the belief that compositors reproduced the spelling of their copy. But a preponderance of "murther" and "shew" spellings in the Folio, for instance, was merely due to the fact that Jaggard *A* and *B* preferred these spellings to "murder" and "show"—and compositors' preferences tell us nothing about the writer's.... All that seems clear is that, in the metamorphosis of manuscript into print, compositors largely followed their own orthographical bent and that the trade showed no inclination to make spelling more phonetic...so that when Jaggard *A* and *B* substituted "murther" for "murder", as they usually plainly did, they were not expressing anything more than a preference for

Notes

one *spelling* over another.... In accidentals, as in substantive read-ings, we need to be chary of supposing that compositors reproduced copy with the conservatism that has sometimes been assumed.'

2 See, for example, Arthur Brown, *op. cit.* *S.B.*, VIII (1956), 19–22; and Alice Walker, *S.B.*, VII (1955), 9.

PAGE 133

1 In what follows I confine my remarks to Elizabethan dramatic texts printed before 1660. Clearly there is little or no applicability to Middle English texts, or to such texts as Spenser, where modernising cannot be contemplated.

2 For instance, some modernising editors will insert every elision in verse that seems to be required, but others will follow the copy-text on the grounds that it is not known whether unelided forms in the original represent slurring or syncopation. In either case anomalies cannot be avoided in prose (see fn. 2, p. 131). An editor may be diffident about normalising elisions, since he cannot tell what were the author's intentions except as revealed by the ordinarily inconsistent copy-text. Yet in following the copy-text's inconsistencies it is often demonstrable that he is only preserving compositorial characteristics (see fn. 1, p. 132).

PAGE 134

1 In many cases common doublets are certainly authentic; in some cases it is evident that a:o and a:u variants are composi-torial misreadings, or errors in the text in question, even though linguistically the forms are possible. In extreme cases linguists have delved deep into obscure dialects in Middle English in order to 'explain' or certify an assumed Elizabethan form that was almost certainly a misprint. That a linguistic form was possible does not in all cases make it probable in dramatic texts. As only one example, for a courtly gentleman on the Elizabethan stage to use a rough dialect form without intent would—on what evidence we have—sound as odd to his audience as would the equivalent today.

1 Anyone who examines very scrupulously the rationale of the modernising process will learn to abandon logic and consistency. This is not the place to discuss the numerous specific problems of modernisation; nor, no doubt, can absolute rules be laid down as guides to ensure uniformity of procedure among editors. For example, if phonological distinctions are to be preserved when used for a specific purpose by the author, we may perhaps sacrifice *banket* for *banquet* cheerfully enough; but what of Beatrice's *berrord* for *bearward*? Is the colloquialism of her pronunciation (if that is what it is) to be preserved as a significant feature of the author's intention, in the same class as *'em* for *them* or *ye* for *you*? Or would any young and lively stage 'gentlewoman' pronounce the word *berrord* even though the manuscript copy of the player's part spelled it *bearward*? If so, what price distinguishing *berrord* from *bearward*? What of all the puns that linguists, rightly or wrongly, are exposing as possibilities? How many times will the linguistic estimate here of an author's intention, and the preservation of an assumed phonetic distinction reflected in the orthography of the original, actually foist a pun on a helpless author regardless of context or propriety —literary matters that our linguistic critics do not always consider? One may repeat, possibility is not probability.

To expose difficulties is not to attack the method, of course; nevertheless, editors engaged in modernisations of texts would be well advised to discuss their difficulties more fully in print for their mutual advantage and the formulation of some working conventions that will do the least damage. The guidance that single editors of recent Elizabethan series have received from general editorial instructions both in England and in America has certainly been insufficient.

2 *Editorial Problem*, p. lii. The belief that, in general, authorial punctuation filters through the compositor and into a print on the same basis as the spelling vitiates in large part the conclusions of most critics who invite us to contemplate subtle authorial intentions manifested in the fine details of the pointing system.

Notes

It is quite true that in *The Virgin Martyr* the compositor seems to have reproduced with some faithfulness Dekker's hyphenation, and the proportion of dashes and of exclamation marks in the Dekker scenes is higher than in the Massinger scenes. However, marks like queries, exclamations, hyphens, and dashes might be expected to impress themselves more strongly upon a compositor than lighter marks. Evidence is not lacking that in certain circumstances an author's punctuation could be reproduced. For instance, Edward Knight's hand is suspected in some of the stage-directions in *The Two Noble Kinsmen* (1634) because of the reproduction in the print of his characteristic colons. I have myself observed in a few Dekker plays the frequent hyphenation found in the scenes in *The Virgin Martyr* and also what I take to be an authorial habit of separating the clauses or phrases of a series by colons. One would suppose that an acceptable and fairly heavy system of manuscript punctuation would more likely be reproduced, at least in part, than an extremely light and erratic one (like that in *The Welsh Embassador* manuscript) that called for constant compositorial judgement. In some cases, it must not be forgotten, the system of pointing may be subject to bibliographical explanation: for instance, some printers' cases seem to have been very short indeed of semi-colon sorts, thus limiting the number that could be set despite the manuscript markings and, in fact, seemingly getting some compositors out of the habit of using semi-colons, except perhaps to relieve a shortage of colons.

PAGE 137

1 The added attraction to some editors may have been the fancied security afforded in cases of doubt. If the modification is ambiguous, for instance, it seems much the easier path to keep the original (ambiguous) punctuation and let the reader decide what modification he prefers. That this procedure is an abnegation of editorial responsibility even for an old-spelling editor is not sufficiently recognised. A reader is unlikely to know more about the characteristics of a text than an editor; and it is scarcely

fair for an editor to force a reader to make decisions that he has himself declined.

PAGE 138

1 One cannot emphasise too much the common-sense view based on contemporary conditions. The dramatic texts of the time, with such exceptions as Ben Jonson's and possibly some of the closet dramas, were not inscribed under the direction of the author as reading editions. On the evidence, such as it is, many of the prints were set from papers the author submitted to the theatre in the expectation that a scribe would make up a prompt-book from them, and the actors would have had their parts copied in yet another transcriptional process. Any man of the theatre would know that his chances of getting small subtleties of meaning conveyed by punctuation through this process, and then retained in a hard-pressed actor's memory, were practically nil.

PAGE 139

1 I trust I am not unusual in feeling the same anachronism, and a consequent disjointedness in my reactions, when in some of the early twentieth-century 'classic' old-spelling texts the editors chose to modernise the pointing while preserving the other features of the original accidentals. This procedure was adopted at the time from a lack of understanding of the Elizabethan punctuation system that led editors to feel it was so erratic as to be meaningless. Unfortunately, their example sometimes lingers on in days when we know more about the matter. I am far from defending the punctuation of any dramatic quarto as so unexceptionable that it should be preserved as scrupulously as the spelling. On the contrary, the old-spelling editor will need to interfere with the pointing of his copy-text more than with any other feature of its accidentals. But he must do so with taste, and always according to the standards of the time. Ordinarily not much more than occasional touching-up is needed. It may be that printed texts exist so deficient in their punctuation as to require the imposition of a completely new

Notes

synthetic system appropriate for the date, and consistent in spirit with the other accidentals. In my limited experience I have not yet encountered one in print (though I have in manuscript); but if I did, I should have no hesitation in repunctuating according to Elizabethan standards, provided such drastic treatment were actually required to make the text intelligible to the kind of reader I should expect to consult the old-spelling edition.

PAGE 141

1 Of course, the distinction is not always as arbitrary or exact as implied in this statement. To argue that the texture of a literary work has no relation to meaning, and that meaning is confined to what we may loosely call words, is to argue nonsense. Any feature of the texture may influence meaning in a substantive manner, with especial reference to the effect of the punctuation on the transmission of meaning. In my view there is little point in attempting to solve the problem in linguistic terms. The distinction of *substantive* from *accidental* (in Greg's usage) is merely a practical one and so need not be affected by the difficulties of exact linguistic definition. (It is convenient, also, to utilise an intermediate class that may be called *semi-substantive*.) If one inquires who decides which is which, and on what grounds, I should say—the editor, and on grounds of common-sense, not to say expediency. So far as I have been able to determine, linguistic principles that attempt to substitute mechanical for meaningful criteria to attack this particular problem are of no marked benefit to an editor.

2 'The Rationale of Copy-Text', *Studies in Bibliography*, III (1950), 21 ff.; reference may perhaps be made to an application in Bowers, 'Current Theories of Copy-Text, with an Illustration from Dryden', *Modern Philology*, XLVIII (1950), 12–20.

PAGE 142

1 On some occasions the original is essential, as when examination of watermarks must be made, or a test for cancellation and substitution of leaves. But for most bibliographical investigation involving the typesetting and its details—and this is the

major end of biblio-textual inquiry—a faithful facsimile made by some good process will usually prove quite satisfactory enough. The impossibility of meeting assumed bibliographical demands has too often been alleged by non-bibliographers as an excuse for shoddy editing.

PAGE 143

1 Greg, *Editorial Problem*, p. lii, n. 1.

PAGE 144

1 Even granting that no new document may turn up, as happened with *Titus Andronicus* and in part with *1 Henry IV*, the constant assimilation of critical information of all sorts, from bibliographical to sociological, will inevitably lead to the necessity from time to time to sum up afresh in the form of a new text what has been won by scholarship. But the intervals between such recensions will be perceptibly longer if the job is properly done each time.

2 Some grammatical anomalies that must be reproduced at present—as any old-spelling editor is uneasily aware—are as likely to be misprints as possible forms. Most textual critics are inclined to shudder at the thought of a synthetic text in which the accidents of a print are altered to what the editor can demonstrate would have been the forms of a holograph. Nevertheless, we should welcome experiments (in cases when we have enough information about the orthographic characteristics of the manuscript) directed towards normalising divergent forms that can be established as compositorial. For example, if I were an old-spelling editor of *Hamlet* and were convinced that Marcellus' *Illo* was a contamination in Q2–F from Q1, I should feel quite free to alter it to *Hillo* to correspond with Hamlet's answer, which was set from manuscript and presumably reproduced the manuscript form. But to induce proper humility an editor must always recall the various spellings for *sheriff* in Hand D of *Sir Thomas More*.

Notes

1 If a bibliographer is dissatisfied with what seems to have been done by an editor and wishes to attack problems leading to a modification of the editor's theories or practice, it is proper to request him to seek his special evidence in the original documents, or photographs, for he would not dream of doing anything else if he were competent in his discipline.

1 Again one must emphasise that regardless of the bibliographical significance that might attach to such details, the critical edition is not bound to reproduce them, since the editor should have exhausted their significance in the preparation of his definitive text.

2 Many of these the editor will be advised to regularise silently, with a simple preliminary statement that he has treated such and such details in such and such a manner. Some assistance may be found in the procedures recommended in the prefatory statement to *The Dramatic Works of Thomas Dekker*, vol. I (1953), although I am not at all sure now that these go far enough in the direction advocated.

1 Something may no doubt be made of the argument that *s* and long *ſ* are merely different orthographical or typographical forms of the same letter whereas the other forms distinguish different letters. It might follow, therefore, that until the letter *j* came into actual modern use it could scarcely be said to exist, and its use in a text before its existence was regularised constitutes a serious anachronism. On the other hand, if we think in terms of sounds, we can scarcely assert that *j* or medial *v* did not exist until their orthographic and typographic equivalents were regularised. And we must consider, on linguistic grounds, that *u* and *v* or *i* and *j* are true complementary letters; that is, when the old system is operating one cannot be used in place of the other, but their interchange has no linguistic bearing whatever on meaning.

We must also consider that the modern system came in irregularly and that not all manuscript or printed texts are pure in these respects. In the transition period, often, a compositor will be relatively indifferent. Also, before the transition period proper, the pressure of spelling reformers would sometimes cause sharply different usages. One compositor in a text might use one system while a second compositor setting another section might use a different one, as happens in Dekker's *Honest Whore* and his *Magnificent Entertainment*, both in 1604, each printed in part in different houses. Since most Elizabethan dramatic texts were printed in a period in which spelling reformers were concerned with modernisation, manuscripts are often more modern in these respects than the prints, and the prints themselves were not uniform. Hence we may well ask what is gained by the retention of a typographical convention that cannot be defended on grounds of meaning and has only a formal purpose. Any editor can modernise in this respect to the advantage of his general reader, with a note to the interested critic what the practice was in the copy-text. Thereupon the specialist, if necessary, can automatically restore the typographical form of the original document in his mind's eye, just as he now does with long *∫*.